PLAN
TO

PLAN TO

Bill Glass
=&=
James E. McEachern

WORD BOOKS
PUBLISHER
WACO, TEXAS
A DIVISION OF
WORD, INCORPORATED

PLAN TO WIN

Library of Congress Cataloging in Publication Data:

Glass, Bill.
Plan to win.

1. Success. I. McEachern, James E., 1935 –
II. Title.
BJ1611.2.G58   1984   158'.1   84-20912
ISBN 0-8499-0431-5

Unless otherwise indicated, Scripture quotations are from the King James
Version of the Bible. Those marked NKJV are from the New King James
Version, published by Thomas Nelson, Inc., copyright 1982, and used by
permission. Quotations marked NAS are from The New American Standard
Bible, copyright 1960, 1962, 1968, 1971 by the Lockman Foundation. Quotation
marked LB is from *The Living Bible, Paraphrased*, copyright 1971 by
Tyndale House Publishers, Wheaton, Ill.

Printed in the United States of America

BILL: To Fred Smith, my mentor and friend.

JIM: To Spencer Hays, who believed in me enough to give me opportunity and who taught me how to take advantage of it.

CONTENTS

THE STORY
BEHIND THIS BOOK

A Word from Bill Glass:

BILL: Jim McEachern was a real winner when I met him several years ago. He was well on his way toward building Tom James, the clothing company he runs, into a $100,000,000 company. His success seemed complete—a great family, an amazing business, a rich and fruitful spiritual life! I was intrigued, because it was obvious to me that this success wasn't an accidental thing. It was studied, almost to the point of being mechanical.

The basic principles that lay behind Jim's winning lifestyle were not new to me. In fact, I had used all these same principles myself, starting even earlier than he had—back when I played professional football with Detroit and Cleveland. I'd even written books, with titles like Expect to Win, *on motivational and success themes.*

But Jim carried the whole thing further. I set goals, but he did it in more detail—writing thousands of pages concerning what his goals were and how he planned to achieve them. I used affirmations. Jim carried his affirmations around on 3 × 5 cards and read them religiously. I listened to motivational tapes, but he listened more often than I did.

I had never met anyone who so completely applied what I believed. Here was a man who applied the princi-

*ples of success with a fierce dedication and methodical
care—and it was working in every area of his life. As
I said, I was intrigued, so I questioned Jim over a period
of several years, and this book is the result! In it, Jim
and I share from our experience some practical ways
the principles of success can be put to work in all areas
of life.*

*Before we actually start talking about these princi-
ples, however, I've asked Jim to tell his own story as
he told it to me. . . .*

The Recipe for Success—Jim McEachern's Story:

*JIM: It was the day after Labor Day, 1964. I was de-
feated, demoralized, and broke—not quite twenty-nine
years old and already a failure. I did not consider suicide, but I thought it might be better if I had never
been born. I had seen the phrase, "born to lose," but I
had never thought it applied to me—until now. I hated
the idea of being a loser.*

*All through July and August of that year I had driven
a snowcone truck in Fort Worth, Texas. I had earned
enough to pay my rent—$12.50 per week—and to buy
groceries. But all summer it had been a day-to-day exis-
tence for my wife, my two children, and me. Driving
the snowcone truck paid about a dollar per hour, and
I had to drive the streets for twelve hours each day to
earn ten or fifteen dollars. Labor Day had been a good
day, but today it seemed that the children who always
appeared when they heard my music box had disappeared from the face of the earth. Of course, they had
not actually disappeared—they were just back in
school.*

*On that first day of school I drove all over the west
part of Fort Worth with my music box blaring, but I
didn't sell many snowcones. As I drove home that night,
I was feeling really low. Most days in July and August
I had been too busy making snowcones to think. But
on that lonely, quiet day, I had had plenty of time to
think. I didn't know what I was going to do, and I was
afraid.*

How had I gotten to this miserable point? Life certainly hadn't started out that way for me. Even though things had been pretty tough for my family during the Depression years, when I was growing up, my earliest memories were mostly positive. I was born 21 October 1935 on a farm in West Texas. There were three houses on that farm. My grandparents lived in the biggest house. My uncle, aunt, and cousin lived in another. My dad, mother, brother, sister, and I lived in the smallest. It was a one-room building that measured only about twelve-by-twenty feet, but as a very young boy I was not concerned about the size of the house I lived in. We always had plenty of good food, because we raised calves, pigs, and chickens, and we grew our own vegetables.

My fondest memories of early childhood were of sitting in my grandmother's lap while she sang and rocked—the rocking chair squeaking in rhythm with the hymns my grandmother sang. My grandmother baked good cookies and chocolate pies and banana puddings. She read the Bible to me and gave me a lot of love.

When I was four years old, my parents decided to get a divorce, so I moved into my grandparents' home. The next ten years were mostly happy years because my grandparents were fine people. They were loving, kind, but firm. My grandmother provided most of the obvious love and kindness while my grandfather provided the firmness.

In the wintertime on the farm there was not much to do. But one day while I was exploring a closet I found an old geography book. I was only five years old at the time, but that book had a profound effect on me. I looked at the pictures each day for hours. I asked my grandmother about the people and the places. I learned about Africa, India, Australia, and South America. I learned to identify many places on the world map. My curiosity was sparked, and a desire to learn was born.

I began my education at a little school at Sparenburg, Texas. The Sparenburg school had twelve grades, with about ten students in each grade. All through elemen-

tary school I was an excellent student. Our school did not have a library, but the county had a bookmobile that came often. I read every book I could get my hands on.

Although my life was pretty good, I did wonder if my dad and mother loved me. Once when I was about ten years old someone told me that my dad had gone to South America and that he was probably never coming back. That hurt, and I worried about him. I did not see either my mother or my dad very often for several years.

As early as the fourth grade, I made up my mind that I was going to go to college. I didn't know anyone who had gone to college, except a couple of guys from my community who had become civil engineers. As a matter of fact, I had no idea what college was like. But I did know I enjoyed learning, and I thought college would be a good place to keep on learning. I continued to be a good student up through the eighth grade.

I lived with my grandparents for ten years, from the time I was four until the year I was fourteen. During those years I had a pretty good self-image. My grandparents gave me a lot of love and encouragement. In addition, I did well in school, and my scholastic success won me respect from the teachers and the other students. A third reason for feeling good about myself was the support of neighbors and relatives. I can still vividly remember the warm feeling I got when they said good things about me.

I was intensely interested in learning while growing up. I read the newspapers diligently and, as a result, I could usually talk about current events with adults. Because of this, one of my neighbors frequently told me, "Someday you're going to be a college professor or a preacher—or you might even be governor of Texas." I had a couple of uncles who really liked to show me off, and so when the family would be together they would ask me questions about world affairs. I would usually know the answers, and they would rave about my unusual gifts. I loved the attention and tried to learn still more.

In the fall of 1949 my grandfather, who by then was

seventy years old, began to suffer failing health. It was difficult for my grandparents to continue to take care of me, my sister, and my brother, so we went to live with my mother and stepfather in Abilene.

After that move, things went downhill fast. My mother was a hardworking lady and was doing the best she knew how at the time, but my stepfather, an alcoholic, made life miserable for me. It wasn't that he abused me. He just didn't give me the emotional support I was used to. My self-image plummeted, and continued to be very poor all through high school. I reached a point where I was failing every course, and I eventually dropped out of school without ever getting a high-school diploma. I went to work in a supermarket.

I had every intention of joining the army in January of 1955. But in the latter part of 1954 a Sunday school teacher urged me to go down to Howard Payne College in Brownwood, Texas, and look over the school. I wasn't at all confident that they would let me in, but at the urging of this teacher I did go down to the school and visit for several days. I took an entrance exam and, to my surprise, they let me enroll. I became a college freshman in January of 1955, several months after my nineteenth birthday.

I really enjoyed college. Howard Payne had a slogan, "The school where everybody is somebody." And for the first time in a long while, I did feel like I was somebody. I made a lot of friends, and knew just about everybody on campus.

I wasn't quite that successful when it came to academics. I would either drop or flunk about one course per semester. But I made a few As and Bs and managed to get along with about a C+ average.

In the spring of 1955 another student asked me if I would like to sell Bibles that summer. I said, "Man, I can't sell anything." He told me there was a man coming from the Southwestern Company in Nashville, Tennessee, and that I ought to at least come by and meet him. I never had met anyone from Nashville, so I decided it would be all right at least to go by and meet him.

At that meeting Mr. Fred Landers, who was the sales

manager for the company, was able to show me that I could do pretty well selling books door-to-door. So in the summer of 1955 I went to Galax, Virginia, and stayed the entire summer selling books, Bibles, dictionaries, cookbooks, and children's books. I did pretty well and had a lot of fun.

I continued in college through May of 1957, but then I ran out of money and had to leave. I found a job in Houston with International Harvester Company. While working there I went to school part time and spent a lot of time with my relatives in Channelview, Texas. While attending church in Channelview I met Arlene Norris. Soon Arlene and I were spending a lot of time together and, on 28 June 1958, she became my wife.

Three weeks after Arlene and I were married, I received a notice from the draft board and, in August of 1958, I was inducted into the army. After basic training I entered medical training and went to the neuropsychiatric section of the Medical Service Corps. That turned out to be a great experience. I learned a great deal about how the mind and emotions work and found the entire subject fascinating. In all, the army was a growing experience for me.

After finishing my stint in the army I reentered Howard Payne in the fall of 1960. This time, because of having had a fairly successful army experience (and probably because I was married and my wife was expecting), I dug in. I was able to hold a forty-hour-a-week job and to take a full load in school. And I made the Dean's List for four semesters! That, in addition to my successful army experience and some pretty good summers of selling books, went a long way toward restoring my damaged self-image.

In the fall of 1962 Arlene and I moved with our baby daughter, Karen, to Post, Texas, where I became a schoolteacher. I enjoyed teaching. The kids were great, and I enjoyed the subject matter. Had the pay been better, I would probably have continued teaching school for a long time. But we could just barely make ends meet, even though we didn't spend extravagantly on anything.

In February of 1963 our second child, Mike, was born. As we paid the doctor bill it became obvious to me that I was not going to be able to provide for my wife and children the way I wanted to. I decided that I would leave teaching and go back to working in a supermarket.

We moved to Fort Worth, and I went to work for the largest supermarket chain in town. I was working in their largest store, and I thought everything was going to be all right. I was happy. I felt good about my job because at last I had an opportunity to get in a position to earn a good living for my family. But then, after working at the supermarket several months, I became pretty good friends with the manager and asked him how much he made. He told me—and I couldn't believe the low figure. I was disillusioned. So I left, and spent the summer of 1964 driving that snowcone truck. It was at the end of that summer that I was faced with the reality that I had come to a dead end.

As I said before, I was twenty-nine, and unhappy— a college graduate, an army veteran, with selling experience and schoolteaching experience. And yet it seemed as if it were all to no avail.

I didn't have a good job; I was just barely eking out a living. I lived with my wife and two children in a small three-room apartment that cost us fifty dollars a month. We had to plan very carefully in order to stretch the grocery money out over a week. I had a car, but it wouldn't run, so each week I had to set aside three dollars solely for bus fare. If I used any of the three dollars for anything else, I'd have to walk to and from work—and it was a long walk!

That fall my self-esteem continued to spiral downward. All my life, my feelings of self-worth had been determined by what other people thought of me. When others treated me well, when I was in an encouraging, loving situation, when my surroundings were favorable, I did well. But when I wasn't treated well or didn't have good surroundings, then my self-image went down. Now it was at an all-time low.

One evening during that fall I idly picked up one

*of my wife's cookbooks and started leafing through the
section on cakes. As I looked through the recipes, it
suddenly dawned on me that the cookbook was a success
book! It gave detailed instructions on how to bake a
cake successfully. It told exactly what ingredients to
use, and how to mix them. It gave precise instructions
about how hot the oven should be and how long the
cake should be left in the oven. It even told what to
do to keep the cake from sticking to the pan!*

*As I read those recipes, I realized that the cookbook
writers didn't leave anything to chance. The instructions were very detailed. And it seemed to me that, even
though I seldom cooked and had never baked a cake, I
could bake a pretty good cake by following those instructions.*

*I remember thinking, "Wouldn't it be terrific if there
was a recipe book for living successfully?"*

*Soon after that, in the middle of my despair, I got
a call from heaven—or at least it seemed so at the time.
The caller was Spencer Hays, a fellow I had met while
selling Bibles for the Southwestern Company in the
summer during my college years. Spencer was planning
to open a new business, and wondered if I would be
interested in working with him.*

*I was so excited at the glimmer of hope that I did
not even bother at first to find out what kind of business
Spencer planned to get into! I just said yes. I wanted
to be around Spencer and learn from him, because I
realized he had been successful in almost every way
in which I was failing.*

*Spencer had a background similar to mine, although
he had excelled at athletics in high school and I hadn't.
During his college years at Texas Christian University
he had become one of the most successful student salesmen ever for the Southwestern Company, and had continued to do well for the company as a sales manager.
He had a good job, a nice apartment, a good car. He
was able to provide for his family. It was obvious to
me that he was respected by a lot of people. (Spencer
has continued to do well to this day. Currently he is
the major stockholder in several businesses that to-*

gether exceed a hundred million in annual sales. Spencer is chairman of the executive committee for both Tom James and the Southwestern Company.)

When Spencer offered me the opportunity to be associated with him, I immediately thought, If I'm around Spencer I can figure out what his recipe for success is. *So I started working with his new company, a custom clothing company called Tom James, in the fall of 1966. At the same time, I started on my own private campaign to discover just what it is that makes the difference between success and failure in life.*

During the remainder of 1966, and most of 1967, I diligently studied the lives of successful people to find out what caused them to be successful. I read books and magazine articles, and I questioned successful people. As I called on men to sell them clothes I asked them, "What is it that has enabled you to do so well?" I also asked, "What's the most important thing you've learned since you've started in business?" In some cases I would ask, "What one thing do you know now that you wish you had known when you first started?" Or I would ask, "If you were going to give advice to some young person just starting out in business who really wanted to do well, what would be the most important bit of advice that you would give?"

What I was doing was seeking the recipe for success. What are the ingredients? How are they put together? How long do they take to be completed? I had become confident while looking through the cookbook that I could bake a good cake. I was now becoming confident that, if I found the recipe for successful living, I could be successful, too. I searched through my notes trying to find the common ingredients—the characteristics that successful people shared.

Then, one day late in 1967, it dawned on me that all the people I had read about and questioned had at least one thing in common. They all had goals. *This shared ingredient had not been obvious to me at first because not all the people I had studied used the same word. Some people said they had "goals" to do this or that, but others talked of having a "vision" of achieving* what they wanted to do. Some called their goals "dreams," and still others used the words, "want to." They might say something like, "Ever since I was a little boy, I wanted to. . . ."

I realized that goal, dream, vision, "want to," and ambition were just different words for the same process. When I recognized that this was something all successful people go through, I took a sheet of paper and wrote at the top of it this question: "What are my goals?" And then I began to list what I wanted most out of life.

That was just the beginning. But it was the beginning of a whole new life for me—a life of being a success instead of a failure, of being the kind of person I really wanted to be. As I learned the process of setting and working toward goals, I also learned about some of the other "ingredients" of success—and about how those ingredients could become part of my life. And I learned that the same basic ingredients of success apply to all areas of life—not just business.

In this book, Bill Glass and I would like to share with you the ingredients we have discovered to be important in a recipe for life. The basic ideas aren't original, but what we say about "mixing the ingredients" is extremely personal and based on our own experience. It has worked for us—let it work for you!

PLANNING

"We should make plans—counting on God to direct us."
—Proverbs 16:9, LB

Let's suppose you want to build a building. You know exactly what you want in your building. You want a certain look. You have definite ideas about how tall the building will be and how much floor space there will be. How do you convey what you want to another person? You start drawing and diagraming, and writing down every detail. The building is to have ten floors. Each floor is to have twelve thousand square feet. You want it to be primarily brick and glass. You want rest rooms for both men and women on each floor.

At one point perhaps you look over your plans and suddenly realize, "There is no way to get from the bottom to the top! It would not be practical to take a helicopter to the tenth floor. We have to put elevators and stairways in the plans." You continue studying the plans to see what else you may have forgotten.

After a great deal of effort devoted to diagrams and drawings you can pretty well describe to the architect what you want your building to be like. Then he can actually draw up plans to specifications for a building that will have the proper structural strength. Since you're not an engineer or architect, you don't know exactly how much steel it might need and what kind of foundation it would require. You just know what kind of building you want when it's finished. You convey all this information to the architect, and he puts it in blueprint form so the builders can actually construct it.

A Blueprint for Your Life

It is obvious that you must have a detailed plan for a building. But many people don't realize that it is even more important for every person to have a *life plan*—a written "blueprint" for the kind of life he or she wants. Who should establish written life plans? Everyone should—doctors, lawyers, salespeople, students, teachers, ministers, housewives, mothers, dads. Everyone needs to get a picture of the direction he wants his life to take. And to be really helpful the picture should be drawn in detail.

We recommend spending at least thirty minutes a day writing on your blueprint—choosing priorities, setting goals, thinking of ways to achieve your goals, reviewing your progress on goals you have already set. Obviously, you will accumulate hundreds of pages. And slowly you will develop a well-defined picture of the direction your life is taking.

Some people think that it is more "spiritual" just to be spontaneous. But God can lead us in the process of planning just as he can in spur-of-the-moment decisions. And Christ encouraged us to plan precisely. He said, "Which of you, intending to build a tower, sitteth not down first, and counteth the cost . . . ?" (Luke 14:28).

Starting with Priorities

Dallas Cowboys head coach Tom Landry once said that he has three major life focuses: God, family, and profession. Another way of saying this is that those three areas of his life, in that order, are his top priorities. We think this idea of priorities is a good place to start in formulating a life plan. Before specific goals are set, it is helpful to decide what areas of life are most important to you. This is something each person has to decide for himself. But we believe Coach Landry's choice of priorities is very sound, and very biblical.

Matthew 22:37 reads, "Thou shalt love the Lord thy God with all thy heart, and with all thy soul, and with all thy mind." Jesus said, "This is the first and great [most important] commandment" (v. 38), meaning that God should be the number-one emphasis of our lives. We should love him with all our heart, soul, and mind. And in Ephesians 5:25 Paul writes, "Husbands, love your wives, even as Christ also loved the church, and gave himself for it." In the next chapter of Ephesians, Paul says to fathers, "Bring them [your children] up in the nurture and admonition of the Lord" (Eph. 6:4). We believe Coach Landry is on sound footing when it comes to his priorities because we believe the Bible clearly puts God in first place, with the family in a strong second place to God.

JIM: My wife and I made the decision early in our life together to focus our time, energy, ability, and attention on our family. This was because we realized that one day our children would be adults, and that the kind of adults they were going to become depended much on what kind of parents they had. We didn't want our children to be fearful. In fact, one of the most important things we wanted to teach our children was not to be afraid to try!

Another thing we wanted to teach our children was not to care too much what other people think. Now, that may sound arrogant, but we didn't want them to be susceptible to peer pressure. They must do something not just because other people are doing it, but because it is right. We didn't want our children to let criticism affect them. A person who lets criticism destroy him is always going to be down in the dumps, because someone is always going to be putting him down.

We didn't want rejection to bother our children. We wanted them to know what love is, and we wanted them to know that they were loved. We concentrated on helping to make sure they would grow up without some

*of the problems we had faced. We weren't trying to shield
them from problems; we were trying to show them how
to deal with problems. And we wanted to shield them
from self-induced problems. There's no point in getting
into trouble just so you can learn how to get out of
it!*

A Fourth Priority

*BILL: Tom Landry said, "If it doesn't benefit my rela-
tionship to God, my family, or my business, then I'm
not going to do it." Those are the three priorities on
which he has based his life plan. I agree with him, but
I would add a fourth priority: taking care of our health.
The body needs trimming up and exercising. It needs
the right kinds of foods and the right amount of health-
ful sleep.*

Essentially, then, we're borrowing from the great coach
and then adding an idea of our own when we say that,
in our view, a successful life plan would involve doing
only those things that benefit our relationship to God,
our family, our profession, or our health.

That sounds selfish—as if we were only going to do
what is good for us personally. But look more closely.
If we're doing what benefits our relationship to God, that
is not selfish. That's not attention turned inward, but
rather attention turned outward, toward God. When we
do what is best for our family, we are not focusing attention in on ourselves, but giving attention to them. If we're
doing what benefits our profession, we are also helping
everybody in the organization we work for and all the
people that organization touches—which could mean thousands. That's not selfish!

The fourth priority—our health—is necessary if we are
to take care of these higher priorities. Without health,
we can't do anything! Taking care of our health doesn't
take much time—only fifteen or twenty minutes of good
exercise each day, seven to eight hours of proper rest,
and eating the right kinds of food. It doesn't take any
longer to eat properly than it does to wolf down junk
food!

WRITING YOUR GOALS

Setting general priorities is only the first step of developing a blueprint for your life. Those priorities are crucial, but they are still only general categories. Developing a blueprint for your life means writing out specific, personal goals: spiritual goals, your family goals, your business goals, and your health goals. One good way of doing this is to put each goal on a separate sheet of paper in a notebook. Under each goal write out the reason the goal is important to you. Then, on the same sheet of paper, write down all your ideas as to how to achieve that goal. It may take years to accumulate all the information you need about how to achieve your biggest and most important goals. But the process of writing down ideas as they occur to you and reviewing them periodically will keep you moving toward your goals.

The best way to keep your goals constantly on your mind is to write them on 3 x 5 cards and to read your cards every day. Your goal cards will help keep you focused on what is really important to you and help keep you from wasting your time on activities that don't help you achieve any of your goals. It is also a good idea to read often what you have written in your notebook about how you plan to achieve your goals. You may want to revise these strategies as your situation changes. That is fine, as long as you keep your basic priorities and goals in mind.

SET HIGH GOALS

A good principle to remember in setting goals is to *aim high from the beginning.* Many people are reluctant to set high goals because they think that, if they don't reach the goal right away, they will have failed. That is the wrong definition of failure. Failure does not mean being unable to reach a goal quickly. Failure means not trying to achieve something that is important. As long as you are learning, trying, and improving, you are making progress. If you are making regular progress toward your worthwhile, predetermined goals, you are successful. The

important word is progress. The time isn't important. You
may have to try a hundred times. It's important not to
be too tough on yourself. Give yourself some time. Keep
on trying. Never give up.

Remember, people seldom achieve beyond their goals.
Occasionally, you may achieve something by accident, but
you won't be able to repeat the achievement. On the other
hand, if you achieve your goal, we guarantee that your
achievement won't be an accident!

Another reason we've found that people seem reluctant
to set high goals, is that they're afraid of what other
people will think. You may think, *If I set a high goal,
people are going to think I'm crazy.* In that case, don't
tell them!

*JIM: Back in 1967, when I first made the discovery
that most successful people set goals, I sat down and
wrote down some goals for myself. One of these had
to do with my business. I wanted to help build Tom
James to $100,000,000 in sales. Now, at the time I wrote
that goal down, Tom James had not yet sold $200,000
worth of clothes in a single year! We had only been
in business a year, and had sold $20,000 or $30,000 worth
of clothes in those final four months of 1966. In 1967,
I knew that we were going to sell close to $200,000 worth
of clothes—only one fifth of a million. And yet there I
was writing down that my goal was to help build our
little $200,000 company into a $100,000,000 giant.*

*I told several people about my goal, and most of them
laughed. How could I in my wildest dreams think of
selling $100,000,000 worth of clothes when we were a
long way from selling a million—or even a quarter million? Of course, not everybody ridiculed the idea. When
I first talked to Spencer Hays about my $100,000,000
goal, he listened with interest. I don't recall his saying
anything specifically encouraging or discouraging, but
I took his listening as evidence of approval. I knew that
if he thought I were wrong he would tell me.*

*After having quite a number of people laugh and only
a few people encourage me, I quit telling very many
people about my goal. I didn't give it up; I just quit
telling most people. (Obviously, I kept reminding people*

*in the company about it; they are to this day pivotally
involved in its realization.) And we are achieving our
goal.*

In the long run, does it really make all that much difference what people say? Both of us have tried to have the
attitude that we honestly don't care what anyone else in
the world thinks about us. We obviously have lapses, times
when we get too caught up in pleasing other people, but
we try not to really care what other people think. You
could say, "That's really a bad attitude; it could result
in irresponsibility." But if we care how we act toward
other people, we won't have an antisocial attitude, even
if we don't care what people think about us.

The important thing is to care about others, not about
what others think. If you have love toward people, they
will probably think well of you. But it doesn't really matter
if they don't. The important thing is doing what you know
to be right.

The man in all history who was most concerned about
what people thought was Pilate. The Bible tells us that
he knew Christ to be innocent. He didn't want to crucify
him. The Bible says in Mark 15:15, "So Pilate, willing to
content [please] the people . . . delivered Jesus . . . to
be crucified." He was a real "people pleaser," but he was
hated by the people and even lowered in his own self-
esteem. And of course, this doesn't even take into consider-
ation the most important opinion of all—God's! If we always try to please people, chances are we'll end up
displeasing God and not respecting ourselves.

Sometimes it's the people who love us most who try
to discourage us from setting high goals for ourselves.
That's because they want us to be cushioned from disappointment. If you don't set a high goal, they think, then
you won't be disappointed. But then you won't ever
achieve much, either.

GOALS ARE FOR EVERY AREA OF LIFE

You may think that goal-setting is only for big projects,
like making a hundred million dollars in sales or winning

the Super Bowl. But the process of planning and goal-setting applies to all areas of your life. When she was a teenager, Jim's daughter, Karen, set a goal to earn "first chair" in the flute section of the Irving High School Band. That goal motivated her to practice faithfully and diligently for hours each day. The practice enabled her to develop her talent and to achieve her goal. We know another high-school girl who has made it her goal to earn an academic scholarship. This goal gives her meaning and purpose as she attends class and does her homework.

Every area of your life deserves worthwhile, predetermined, written goals. Without specific goals, people tend to wander aimlessly in their lives. Unless goals are written down, they are often forgotten. The more clearly you define what you want to achieve, the more likely you are to achieve your desired objective.

We have suggested four areas of life in which to set goals: your spiritual life, your family, your business, and your health. You may have numerous goals and plans in each of these areas. And there are many other areas you may want to develop: your character, your education, your finances, your leisure time, and various other individual interests. But it is important to establish the order of priority for all your goals, because some are obviously more important than others.

Working Toward Your Goals

Once you have written down your goals and your plans for achieving them, the process of working toward those goals is continual. You need to be always checking your cards, looking over your notebook, reviewing your goals. Consistently do the things that are going to improve your self-image. Constantly say and do the things that are going to cause you to have a better attitude toward God, your family, and your job. Always do the things that will cause you to have a better attitude toward the people with whom you come in contact. Strive every day for improvement. Don't care too much about what other people think. But do care about how you act toward other people, and how you treat them.

One helpful way of approaching your really big, hard-to-achieve goals is to break them up into smaller, easier goals. Then you can focus on each of these smaller goals at a time and gradually work toward the larger goal.

JIM: When I first set my goal to help Tom James achieve $100,000,000 in sales a year, I knew my goal was very high. But I broke that stupendous possibility into short-term goals. In 1968, for instance, our goal was to sell $284,000; in 1969, it was to sell $400,000; in 1970, $568,000; and in 1971, $800,000. Every two years I wanted our sales to double. In 1973, our goal would be $1,600,000; in 1975, $3,200,000; in 1977, $6,400,000; in 1979, $12,800,000; in 1981, $25,600,000; in 1983, $51,200,000; and in 1985, $102,400,000. Every year would see an approximate 42% increase over the year before. We have been able to achieve our larger goal by achieving one smaller goal after another.

ACHIEVING WORTHWHILE GOALS TAKES WORK

Developing a blueprint for your life and working to achieve your goals can be a fulfilling and worthwhile process, but it's not easy. Personal initiative is an essential ingredient in achieving your goals. Mary Crowley, one of the nation's most successful businesswomen, told a student group on a university campus recently to adopt this ten-word motto: "If it is to be, it is up to me." That's an important phrase to remember when it comes to your life plan.

Tom Landry once said during a television interview, "As coach, I have to make the players do what they don't want to do in order to achieve what they want to achieve." To achieve your goals, you need to be a tough coach for yourself. At times, it will be necessary to make yourself do what you do not want to do in order to achieve what you do want to achieve. Jesus did not want to be crucified, but he went obediently to the cross to redeem sinful man from the penalties of sin. As Jesus was about to be betrayed, he prayed, "O my Father, if it be possible, let this cup pass from me: nevertheless not as I will, but as thou wilt" (Matt. 26:39).

At times when you get discouraged, when you do not seem to be progressing, review the reasons why your goal is important to you. A top salesman, Ash Deshmukh, says that every goal you set ought to be one to which you are emotionally committed. If you have a powerful emotional reason for each of your goals, you can combat the emotions caused by the rejection and disappointment you encounter as you strive to achieve your goals. Obviously, your life blueprints must relate to your value system, your purpose in life. We will discuss this in greater detail in another chapter.

GOAL SHEET

What is my goal?

Why is this goal important to me?

How can I achieve this goal?

PICTURING

One big difference between winners and losers is imagination. And imagination is not just a matter of intelligence. It's not just a way of thinking. It's more a matter of learning to "see" with our "inner eyes"—learning to comprehend a reality that is bigger than what we can take in through our five senses. It's the ability to visualize what *can* happen as clearly as what has happened in the past and what is happening now. George Bernard Shaw said, "Some people see things as they are and wonder why. I see things as they have never been and ask 'why not?'" That's imagination.

Just what is reality, anyway? Most people say it is that which we can see with our eyes, hear with our ears, touch, taste, or smell. Actually, that which is permanent is not just what we identify with our senses. What we experience with our senses will not last. It will change. Things that have happened in the past are gone, with only a gravestone or monument to mark the most important of people or events.

"You do not know what will happen tomorrow. For what is your life? It is even a vapor that appears for a little time and then vanishes away" (James 4:14, NKJV). So what's more real—that which is now, or that which is past? What's more real—that which is now or that which is future? That which we see with our inner eyes can be just as real as what we can see with our outer eyes!

SEEING WITH OUR INNER EYES

One of the reasons some people have been able to break loose from the average is that they have learned to see with their inner eyes—and to believe in what they see. Average people don't exercise their imaginations. All they can see is what "is" or "was." They seldom catch a glimpse of what can be.

It is natural for children to use their imaginations. But as people get older, they tend to become inhibited or maybe too busy, and they don't use their imaginations properly. Often they stop using them at all! Children have fantastic imaginations and they utilize them. That is one of the reasons why children grow and progress so quickly. We're convinced that adults become stale and stagnant to just about the same degree that they stop using their imaginations.

So how do you learn to use your "inner eyes"? The best way is to set aside a period of time every day to practice exercising your imagination. Find a quiet place and close your eyes so that you are not distracted visually. You need to be in a room with a comfortable temperature, because if you're too hot or cold you will have a harder time concentrating on what you're imagining. (The things that are most likely to intrude on our inner pictures are the things which we come to know through the five senses. Unfortunately, these are also the things that are usually of less importance.)

Once you have gotten comfortable and closed your eyes, try to blank out all your thoughts. Then concentrate on a specific subject—a goal or a future situation. Try to picture it in detail, over a period of time. Then write down a description of what you have pictured.

BILL: This training of the inner eyes is something that comes very naturally for some people. For others, it is a little more difficult, but it's possible for everyone.

This is the way I did it when I was playing professional football for the Cleveland Browns. I would sit in a room and imagine myself having a huge screen lowered before me. On that screen I would try to picture myself playing football—perhaps an upcoming game. But I would try to make that picture appear in 3-D living color! I tried to get the sights, sounds, and everything I would feel on that screen. I would imagine myself charging across the line and into the tackle. I'd feel the opponent's body quivering beneath my blow and feel him falling down on the inside as I rushed to the outside to throw the quarterback for a loss. I would go over all the possibilities of what might develop during the game—one situation at a time. And I would write down on a sheet of paper everything I imagined. I would repeat this process continuously until what I had imagined was burned into my mind.

This practice of imagining or visualizing can be helpful no matter what you do—whether you are a public speaker, doctor, lawyer, student, scientist, schoolteacher, parent, salesman, or whatever. In fact, it could make the difference between success and failure. Imagine yourself accomplishing all your goals on a daily basis. Put emphasis and time on imagining yourself accomplishing your major objectives, but not in a general or abstract way. Be very specific. See yourself reaching those goals in a step-by-step manner.

Setting aside a regular time to "practice" imagination is an invaluable habit. But don't limit yourself to that time. Practice positive imagining all day long. Every time a picture of yourself floats through your mind, make certain it is a picture of a winner. If a negative picture comes into your mind, replace it with a positive picture of yourself doing what you want to do like a superstar! If you should see yourself fumbling a football, go back and picture yourself carrying the ball flawlessly. If you should imagine yourself missing a deadline, replace that picture in your mind with a picture of yourself getting the job done ahead of time. If you see yourself making a social mistake, replace it with a picture of yourself doing extremely well in that social situation.

THINKING IN PICTURES

You see, the mind thinks in pictures. Those pictures are programmed into the computer of your subconscious, and they have a powerful effect to either be successful or to fail.

BILL: I recently read an interesting article that illustrates the strong effect pictures can have on us. According to the article, a baby who is born too early is often separated from its mother and put in an incubator or on a respirator, while the mother either stays in her hospital room or goes home. The baby needs its mother's milk, because the milk is easier to digest than formula and helps fight infection. But since the baby is not there to nurse, the mother often has difficulty producing milk, even with a breast pump. She cannot make her milk flow by thinking abstractly, "I want to produce milk for my baby." But hospitals have found that, if the mother looks at a picture of her newborn, her milk will usually flow freely.

Our minds are activated by pictures. And so are many of our physiological functions. An attractive woman will arouse sexual desire in a man. A beautiful meal will cause hunger pangs to strike. Pictures motivate us to *do* something (although of course we always have a choice whether or not to take the action we are motivated to do).

This is why using our inner eyes is so important in helping us reach our goals. Picturing ourselves doing a thing successfully conditions our minds for actually doing it like winners. For the same reason, it is extremely dangerous to picture ourselves failing, because once a picture of failure is in our minds it becomes difficult to keep from failing. Remember, the mind operates by pictures!

If you are in a leadership position (a parent, teacher, coach, or manager), make sure you always picture those under your leadership as winners. Treat them as winners—talk to them as winners. Even when they "mess up," hold on to the positive picture of them.

JIM: It just scared me silly to think that it was possible for my children to fail in reaching their potential! So I started thinking, Now what can I do to help them become exceptional adults? I'd picture my children be-

*coming bold, confident, and determined—mature, re-
sponsible achievers. I made lists of what I would do to
help them become just that. (The first thing on the list
was to get my wife's help!) You know, my children are
turning out almost exactly as I thought. I'm convinced
that, if my wife and I hadn't created an environment
that reinforced positive images, they would have been
much less than the wonderful people they are!*

*I can't emphasize enough how important the process
of picturing has been in every area of my life. With
my inner eyes I tried to picture the kind of Christian
I was going to be, the kind of father I was going to be,
the kind of businessman I was going to be. Do you realize how difficult it was for me in 1967 to put down
on a piece of paper that I was going to help build a
$100,000,000 company when Tom James had only
$200,000 in total sales? Was that number realistic? Yes,
but coming up with it took imagination. I didn't just
pick a number out of thin air and say, "That's realistic." I had to sit down and think about it and practice
visualizing.*

*Over a period of time, as I did this, the $100,000,000
goal became more real in my mind than whatever
the actual sales were. If a person asked, "How big is
your company?" my automatic response would be,
"$100,000,000." In the early years I had to say, "Now,
wait a minute, Jim. We are not actually at that point
yet." I knew this, but with my inner eyes I still had
to view my company in terms of my goal for it.*

That's how powerful learning to see with your inner
eyes can be—what you visualize can come to seem more
real than what is actually going on in your life at present.
That doesn't mean you should become oblivious to reality.
Obviously some areas of life, such as age, require realism;
when someone says, "How old are you?" you give them
your present age, not the age you would like to be. But
sometimes it is necessary to change your practical realism
in order to free up your imagination.

Using your inner eyes needs to be a regular part of
the time you spend working on your life plan. Discipline
yourself to sit down every day for a period of time to

picture yourself reaching your goals. Visualize your goals as if they were present reality. See yourself as a winner. Make your picture include complete detail.

Try to avoid getting hung up on how long your goals are going to take. Nobody who sets a goal knows exactly how long it will take to gather the information required to achieve the goal. Nobody knows how much thought must be focused, or how much work must be done, to achieve the goal. But goals can be achieved—even seemingly impossible ones. When John F. Kennedy first proposed landing an American on the moon, such a venture seemed preposterous, but it was accomplished within the decade.

JIM: I certainly didn't know enough in 1967 to successfully manage a multimillion-dollar company. However, because I established an ambitious goal, believed in it, pictured it, and sought ideas about ways to achieve it, the information came almost like a flood.

Having a goal that is not yet achieved creates a certain tension. There are two ways to get rid of this tension. One is through the achievement of your goal, and the other is through escape. You know what most people do? They escape. They lay aside their goals and quit thinking about them because thinking about the goals creates pressure. They bury their goals to avoid the heat.

I think that's the loser's way out! I'd rather go ahead and be a little uptight in order to become something better. There's no change, improvement, or growth without this tension. So, personally, I'd prefer to face the pressure and have the success that follows.

USING OUR MINDS

Napoleon Hill and W. Clement Stone, in their book, *Success through a Positive Mental Attitude*, make the statement, "Whatever the mind of man can conceive and believe, the mind can achieve." We both read that statement and liked it, but we found ourselves asking, "What does this mean? Why is it important to us? How can we use it?" It dawned on us that we didn't completely understand what it meant.

So we started asking some other people, "Do you believe that 'whatever the mind of man can conceive and believe, the mind can achieve'?" "Well, certainly I do." "Would you tell us what it means?" we asked. We never got a satisfying answer.

So we asked ourselves, "What does the word *conceive* mean?" The thing that came to mind immediately was the conception of a baby. When the sperm of a man joins with the egg of a woman, a baby is conceived. Those two cells already know what color hair and eyes the baby will have. Just two cells! They know to put five fingers on each hand and five toes on each foot, and they know how tall the person will be as an adult. In those microscopic cells is a total and complete blueprint for a human adult. The physical appearance down to the most minute detail is implanted there. Even family personality traits are blueprinted in those two cells.

BILL: My father died when my sister was less than two years old. She has no memory of him. Yet she is so like him it is almost laughable. The shape of her toenails, her personality, her traits and tendencies are almost identical to his. She couldn't possibly have learned these things from her environment; they must have been blueprinted in her genes from the moment of her conception.

We concluded that must be the meaning of the word *conceive* as it is used in the statement from *Success through a Positive Mental Attitude.* It refers to making a complete, detailed blueprint of the finished product. To be really useful, a life plan or blueprint for life needs to be just as thorough a blueprint as those two cells at the moment of conception. All the goals need to be spelled out in detail, and the plans for carrying out those goals need to be specific. If the blueprint is complete, then the results will be exact, no matter how complex the structure.

To make a life plan that is a thorough blueprint for the future, imagination is essential. We must be able to visualize the finished product, and to imagine all the steps that must be taken to achieve it. That's what is done with the blueprint for a building; right there on paper is exactly what needs to be done to construct the building. Similarly, a life blueprint should show exactly what must be done to achieve the goals that have been set. As we list the things that are necessary to reach the objective, the blueprint becomes more complete and more detailed—and easier to believe in and follow.

Obviously, the technique of planning we're talking about has to be adapted to the desired result! It is one thing to build a company, for instance, and another to train a son. When you are building a company, you can have extremely detailed plans. But when you are bringing up a son, you are dealing with an eternal soul that has choices of his own. The child must be allowed to choose for himself. As he grows older, his freedom is increased until adulthood, when you become simply an advisor and an encourager. When he is young, your supervision is close and important. You seek to keep in mind a picture of what you want him to become, and to do only those things that will fit the blueprint of the individual you want him to become. Proverbs 22:6 says, "Train up a child in the way he should go: and when he is old, he will not depart from it." Here is a Bible promise that if the child is properly "blueprinted," the kind of adult he becomes is predictable. Even the "old" (mature) man is not going to depart from the training, according to this promise!

BILL: Jim, I've noticed something about all four of your children. The pictures in their minds must be just like the one in yours. This is not just teaching; it is training. Training is something that is done with a parent's total life. The parent shows the child what he wants him to be like by modeling it in his own life and by pointing it out in others. Slowly, through the years, the picture will be transfered from the parent's mind to the child's. Then the child is truly trained— ". . . he will not depart from it."

Jim, you and your wife have been excellent trainers!
Visualizing must be done if a person is going to achieve very much. So take some time every day for ideas to come. You must picture what can be in as much detail as possible. You need to get a picture of what you want to become. And remember to write down all your ideas. As we mentioned in the previous chapter, we recommend spending

at least thirty minutes a day working on your blueprint. Slowly there will evolve a more well-defined picture of all your goals. Working on your plan and imagining it being carried out could be called *mental conception,* and this is even more important to your success or failure than your original physical conception.

PRAYING

But it's not enough just to visualize what you want to become. That simply conditions the mind. You need to spend meaningful time in prayer, as well. Then God will sharpen all your abilities that he created, and empower you to accomplish infinitely more than you think you can.

You may think you don't have time in your busy schedule to fit in time for exercising your inner eyes. But the reverse is true! When you spend time in picturing, writing, and praying about what you want to become, you will be able to accomplish much more in the time you have left.

BILL: I've met two great visualizers in my lifetime. Both had a constant and fertile production of pictures going in their brain. Both had a semi-mystical quality about them. Both had absolute belief in the success they pictured long before that success was a reality. Both achieved the ultimate of success in their businesses. And both have served as inspirations to me.

One of these was Jim Brown, the legendary running back who was my teammate on the Cleveland Browns. Jim was an absolute natural at this way of thinking. As a child, he simply discovered the way his brain worked—through pictures—and he came to understand the importance of feeding it the right pictures. I lost touch with Brown after we both left football, so I really don't know if he still applies this way of thinking to other areas of his life.

However, I have followed extremely closely the second great visualizer. I've seen him apply not only this principle, but all the others in this book, with astounding success. You've guessed it—the second of these two great visualizers is Jim McEachern. He did it totally by rote at first. His background was against it. He only started after he was already a mature adult failure. But now, in my opinion, he has progressed far beyond most everyone because that which at first felt so strange to him became second nature.

The object in learning to use your inner eyes is to learn how the brain works—through pictures! Then feed the brain only positive pictures, because it will react to the negative pictures just as readily as it does to the positive. Your subconscious is an obedient servant carrying out to the letter what the conscious feeds it. It is like a computer. It can only do what it is programmed to do!

You have heard that "seeing is believing," but faith says that "believing is seeing." In Hebrews 11:1, Paul writes, "Now faith is the substance of things hoped for, the evidence of things not seen." And Proverbs 29:18 tells us, "Where there is no vision, the people perish."

The man or woman who is obviously successful, the one who seems always to come through every situation with flying colors, the one we label "winner," is not that different from everyone else. Winners mess up, make mistakes, and experience tough situations just like everyone else. The difference is in the way they handle mistakes and difficult situations. And the way they handle difficulties partially results from the way they "see."

This is demonstrated clearly in the biblical story of the twelve spies in the wilderness (Num. 13). God had sent Moses to deliver the Israelites from Egypt. He was to lead the people to the Promised Land. As the people approached the Promised Land, spies were sent ahead to check out the situation. The Israelites did not want to move into the area without first checking on the conditions. One man from each of the twelve tribes was selected to be part of this advance party.

It would seem that the twelve would all see essentially the same things, but that was not the case. Ten spies saw giants who would crush them like grasshoppers. But two—Joshua and Caleb—saw a land flowing "with milk and honey." Ten saw problems and even disaster. Two saw opportunity. But the people accepted the report of the ten and responded to the report with fear rather than faith. And because the people let fear determine their actions, they died in the wilderness. Out of the entire adult population only two, Joshua and Caleb, entered the Promised Land.

Even today, too many of us see only the problems in a given situation and therefore respond in fear. Too few see the opportunity and respond in faith.

"Where there is no vision, the people perish. . . ." Vision is essential to life and growth. We like the way Jenkin L. Jones put it: "The vision of things to be done may come a long time before the way of doing them becomes clear, but woe to him who distrusts the vision."

FOCUS

"But one thing I do: forgetting what lies behind and reaching forward to what lies ahead."—Philippians 3:13, NAS

We hear a lot about goals these days. Everyone agrees they are important. But why are they so pivotal? One reason is that goals give us something on which to focus or pinpoint our energies. If we are not focused, our thoughts and energies and efforts will be dispersed. We will scatter-shoot in all directions, and it will be hard for us to accomplish anything really important. We must focus on our goals to utilize our time and ability effectively.

In Philippians 3:13-14, Paul wrote: "This one thing I do . . . I press toward the mark for the prize of the high calling of God in Christ Jesus." There was probably no one in history who had more singleness of purpose than Paul. He focused his whole life on one objective—obeying God. And few people have had quite the impact on the world that Paul has had. In this passage, he was talking of the Christian as one who is in an extremely important race, pressing with everything he has—body, mind, and soul—going flat out for the mark. This is a vivid example of the kind of focus that is necessary to achieve important goals.

How Our Minds Focus

Our brains have a mechanism that is designed to help us focus on and therefore achieve our goals. This mechanism is called the reticular activating system. It is a netlike group of cells at the base of the brain that lets in certain information or stimuli to our conscious minds and cuts out other information. When we are focused on a particular goal, the reticular activating system lets in information that pertains to our goals. It also screens out all sorts of information that could be distracting.

Say, for instance, that you are walking down the street, deeply immersed in an important conversation that relates to your goal. The street noises and even the danger of cars and buses zooming by are cut out by your reticular activating system, and you don't even notice them. (Of course, if you are a normal person with a sense of reality, the reticular activating system would let in the fact that you are getting near the corner and must obey the "Walk" and "Don't Walk" signs. Otherwise, you would get run over, and would never be able to reach your goals!)

Another good example of the way the reticular activating system works can be found in a football game. A wide receiver can run out very far from the rest of the team and still hear the voice of the quarterback, even with thousands of fans yelling at the top of their voices. The running back blocks out all the extra noise. In fact, he doesn't even have to try to do it consciously, because his reticular activating system does it for him.

We see this same thing frequently in the case of young couples who are in love. Sometimes they aren't aware of anyone else in the room, or of normal social graces, because they are so preoccupied. Their reticular activating systems screen out all but their top priority—each other.

There are a great many people who allow too much or too little in through their reticular activating system and whose lives are therefore out of balance. In fact, some people become so immersed in trivia that they become totally unbalanced—even psychotic.

But there are also people who are very well balanced, and who have a beautifully functioning reticular activating system that cuts out things that won't help them achieve their goals. Dallas Cowboys head coach Tom Landry is one of these people. He is completely immersed in his three important objectives—God, family, and business—even to the point that to some he appears preoccupied or cold. But his familiar "deadpan" expression doesn't come from indifference, but simply from being focused. He doesn't allow facial expressions or outward emotional responses to interfere with his concentration on his goal.

WE MUST DECIDE OUR FOCUS

The reticular activating system can be extremely valuable in helping us work toward our goals. But it cannot work for us unless we *have* goals! And the system makes no value judgments. If we have trivial goals, then the system will let in trivial stimuli. Like a camera, the reticular activating system will help us focus our energies and attention. But we are the ones who have to decide on what we are going to focus our time and attention.

JIM: I enjoy taking pictures with my camera. My camera will focus on whatever I want it to. I'm the one who controls where I aim the camera, how much light I let in, and how I turn the lens for distance. When I focus the camera correctly, I get a clean, neat, clear picture. But if I set it on long range and my subject is only two feet away, all I get is a blur.

The camera doesn't care what it is focused on. It is built to take a picture of whatever object I aim it toward, no matter whether that object is important or trivial. Our minds are like that. They don't care what they are focused on. We have the choice of how to focus our time, ability, talent, energy, enthusiasm, and confidence. And if we focus these things on a goal that's really important, our ability to achieve will be magnified.

When we drive, there are many trees, buildings, stores, and other objects along the way that we really don't notice. We just don't see them, because our focus is on the road in front of us, and our reticular activating system is shutting out the things that don't pertain to our goal of driving safely. But we have to *make the choice* to drive safely, to concentrate on our driving instead of on sightseeing or window-shopping. If we try to focus both on the road and on the buildings off to the side, we may have a wreck. We must choose to concentrate on what is most important—our driving—and to shut out the distractions around us.

The same thing is true with photography. We can't take a picture of everything at once! In fact, to take a good picture we have to choose one object to photograph and narrow our focus to exclude almost everything else. But when we do this, we are usually not conscious of deciding what to *exclude*. We choose what to focus on, and then we really don't see the other objects.

HANDLING DISTRACTIONS

All sorts of stimuli compete for our attention constantly. We have eyes to see and ears to hear. We can taste, touch, and smell. And often what we perceive through our senses distracts us toward trivial whims—away from our more important goals.

Say, for instance, that you are on your way to an important appointment. You are thinking about what needs to be accomplished at the meeting and are planning what you will say. But the car radio is blaring, and traffic is heavy. You have a hard time concentrating on your goal of holding a successful meeting.

Any kind of stimuli that distracts from the purpose of your mission tends to scatter your focus. The only question is how much. If you are so distracted that the goal is aborted or poorly achieved, then obviously the distracting factor should be removed, if possible. The radio can be turned off, or you could take a taxi instead of fighting traffic.

BILL: But distractions can't always be turned off as easily as a blaring radio. For instance, during the glory days of the Cleveland Browns I played in four Pro Bowl games and numerous championships. At these events I found it extremely difficult to focus in on my goals. One of the most difficult things about such games for the players is all the hoopla. Hundreds of sports-writers and other news media people converge on the two teams and their coaches. Thousands of fans flock to the city where the contest is to be held, and all this attention makes the whole scene a pressure-cooker. The atmosphere makes focusing on the job at hand well-nigh impossible.

What I always did during these situations was go back to the basics mentally. I would take my "short lists" (lists of those defenses to be used for that game) and begin to picture myself in vivid detail doing my job. Rather than counting sheep at night, I would count myself making sacks on the quarterback. Focusing that way on what I wanted to do helped a lot in handling the distractions.

FOCUS ON WINNING

BILL: Recently I was speaking to the Dallas Cowboys right before they participated in a playoff game for the division championship. I told them, "If I were to place a 2 x 6 plank on the floor and challenge you to walk along it, I would bet every Dallas Cowboy could do it without falling off the board. But if you take that same plank and put it twenty stories up between two build-ings, I would bet that not one Dallas Cowboy would walk the 2 x 6. There might be a few of you who would scoot across on your seats, but none of you would walk across. You might have a lot of guts, but you wouldn't want to prove it by splattering them all over the side-walk below!

"Why is it so much more difficult to walk across the 2 x 6 that is twenty stories up than it is to walk it on the floor? The 2 x 6 is just as wide twenty stories up as it is on the floor. It should be just as easy. The reason is that when it's twenty stories up, you don't focus on walking it. You focus on falling. And that makes walk-ing that 2 x 6 just about impossible."

I continued, "This afternoon, you're going to be twenty stories up, and there will be a hundred million people watching on national television. You'll be under

*tremendous pressure. You will either win and be a great
success, or you'll lose and splatter your guts. One thing
will determine which you will do: what you focus on."*
*The Cowboys went out that afternoon and focused on
winning, and they won big! So will you when you discover the important power of focusing your attention.*

There was a great tightrope walker by the name of
Wallenda. He was one of the greatest tightrope walkers
who ever lived. In 1973 he went down to South America.
While walking between two twenty-story buildings, he
fell to his death. Later in an interview his children were
asked, "Why did he fall? He was seventy-three years old
and had never fallen before. He'd been walking those tight-
ropes almost since he was old enough to walk. Why did
he fall?" They said, "Well, we think it is because about
a week before he fell, he began to talk about falling. It
was the first time we'd ever even heard him use the word
fall. And he did fall!" The great Wallenda is dead today
because he stopped focusing on his objective. When he
focused on walking the rope, he walked it. When he focused on falling, he fell.

FORGET THE PAST

When Paul said, "This one thing I do" (Phil. 3:13), he
was showing singleness of purpose; he was focusing on
his objective. But there's more to that passage in Philippians. One of the secrets of achieving this singlemindedness
is found in what comes right before: "Forgetting those
things that are behind. . . ." The other side to focusing
on winning in the future is learning not to focus on what
has already happened.

*BILL: Fred Smith, my wisest personal mentor, once
told me after he had experienced a business setback:
"I'm like a trapeze artist in the circus. I just turned
loose of one trapeze bar and I dare not look back at
it. If I look back, I may miss the one that's coming at
me right now." Don't get preoccupied with your past
failures or successes. Keep your eyes on your present
objective.*

*Washing embarrassing failures out of your mind
isn't easy. Any similar set of circumstances can trigger*

their recurrence in vivid pictures in your mind. To allow these daydreams of past defeats access to center stage is to assure a repeat performance. But to panic, or to try through willpower to remove these intruders, is a mistake; it usually simply serves to reinforce their impact. It is better to replace these negative mental pictures with positive ones of yourself succeeding.

DON'T SPREAD YOURSELF TOO THIN

A person can do ten, fifteen, or twenty things well. But the more things he tries to include in his life, the more his energy will be diffused. When we spread ourselves too thin, we bring less energy to bear on our main objectives.

Often it will be necessary to focus on several small goals, one at a time, in order to work toward a larger goal. This is like a camera; if you have a roll of thirty-six-exposure film in your camera, you will probably have to focus it thirty-six different times to get thirty-six different pictures. But it's all part of the general goal of taking good pictures.

Similarly, if you are in sales you may have an overall goal of being top salesperson in the company. But your intermediate goals may include getting prospects and lining up appointments, giving your prospects effective presentations, taking care of details effectively, and anything else necessary to getting the results you want. You would focus in on each of these smaller goals one at a time, but you would always keep the larger goal in mind.

This is why we started talking about goals in terms of larger priorities. As we mentioned in a previous chapter, both of us have established these priorities in our lives: glorifying God, benefiting our families, furthering our professions, and maintaining our health. We have personal, specific goals in each of these areas, and we try to focus on these goals. There are lots of things that can take our time and attention which don't do any of those three things, so we just don't do them, because activities that don't work toward our goals simply diffuse our time, energy, and thoughts.

WHAT ABOUT MONEY?

Would you like to make ten times as much money as
you do now? Certainly you would. But we would add a
word of caution here about focusing your energies on
making money. Making money is fine as a motivation,
but it's not really a healthy goal on which to focus. It's
better to focus on doing the things that make the money
for you. For instance, suppose you are in sales. You want
to make money, of course. But the thing that is going
to make the money for you is selling, and the way to
sell is to focus on locating good prospects, lining up appointments with them, and explaining to the prospects
what you can do for them. What is going to make the
money for you is the effort you put into serving people.
You really have to focus on giving products and service
to as many people as you can, and the money will follow.
But if your earnings become your single most important
goal, chances are you won't do well, because you won't
be focusing on giving the service you need to give.

The real trouble with focusing on making money is that
all too often it's just a form of focusing on yourself. And
people who focus their time and attention and energy on
themselves are out of balance and rarely get anywhere.
To take a good picture, you must focus on the object of
the picture, not on yourself. But what many people do
is get their focus off their objective and onto themselves,
and all that does is mess up their lives.

CONCENTRATION MAKES THE DIFFERENCE

Napoleon was once asked, "What is the secret of your
success?" His answer was, "Concentration!" He was able
to concentrate all his attention upon one thing at a time.
He said, "My mind is like a great chest of drawers. I
can pull one drawer out, and look into it intently, and
think only of what is in that drawer. When I have finished,
or have gone as far as I can in concentrating on that
one thing, then I close the drawer and open another. I
stare into it intently until I've exhausted the content of
that drawer, then I close that drawer and open still an-

other. Finally, when the day is done, I close all the drawers and immediately go sound asleep." With this amazing ability to concentrate, Napoleon was able to make history!

One of our favorite baseball heroes—Hank Aaron—has a similar ability to concentrate. He is the all-time home-run-hitting champion—755 home runs! Forty home runs would win the home-run-hitting championship most years, and you would have to hit forty home runs a season for nineteen seasons to hit as many as he did! And he was among the all-time leaders in other categories as well.

One of the things we have heard about Hank Aaron helps explain his success. When he was waiting in the dugout for his turn at bat, he would put his cap over his face. Baseball caps have tiny little airholes with brads around them. He would move his cap in such a way that the pitcher was framed in that little hole and everyone else on the field was blocked out. Then Aaron could study the pitcher's motions. By the time it was Aaron's turn to bat, the pitcher's wind-up, his stance, his every move would have become ingrained into Aaron's subconscious. He got to the point that he knew instinctively what was going to happen when the pitcher threw the ball. He had conditioned his mind to recognize instantly if the pitcher was going to throw a curve ball, change-up, fast ball, or whatever. And he didn't have to think about it; he could react automatically.

Hank Aaron loved fast balls, and he could see them coming in time to react because he had studied the pitcher's motion. When a fast ball came in his alley about chest-high, he would swing, and the ball would usually disappear over the left-field fence. He did this 755 times!

We're convinced that one of the reasons Aaron was able to hit so many home runs was that he focused in on the pitcher's motion to the point that he could almost see the pitcher with his eyes closed! If you've ever hunted all day long, you know that when you close your eyes you see birds. Go to the beach and watch the surf all day, and when you close your eyes you will see the breaking waves. That's the way Aaron concentrated. He didn't just watch the whole ball game; he focused in on something that was pivotal to him—hitting the baseball. If a hitter is going to hit well, he has to react subconsciously. If he has to think on the conscious level, he'll be too slow. But if he has watched that pitcher so intently that the motion is grooved into his subconscious, he reacts with hits. That's what Aaron did.

JIM: What we're saying is to focus your thoughts, energies, time, and abilities on specific goals, and you will accomplish ten times more. I've been able to do this in business. Until age thirty, I was a failure, but then I started to practice focusing. I didn't find any more time, energy, or ability than I had before. I just started concentrating it on a limited number of objectives.

One of the ways we can focus our mind is by reading and reviewing our goals. We both carry our goals, written on 3 x 5 cards, in our pockets. We reinforce our objectives in life by reading those cards every day. Reading your goals helps you focus on the goals more clearly and helps keep you more goal-oriented. Every time you read that card, you will be better able to focus in on your goal.

Focus Magnifies Your Life

JIM: Once, when I was just a boy, I was outside on a rather cold day—it was only thirty degrees Farenheit. I had found an old magnifying glass and was playing with it, catching the rays of the sun in the magnifying glass and focusing them on the ground. Then I focused the rays on an old piece of wood lying nearby. To my amazement, when I focused the rays down to a tiny pinpoint on the board, the wood began to smoke, then to burn. I was able to burn my initials in the board with that magnifying glass. As long as the sun had been diffused over the entire surface of the board, the surface of the wood remained 30 degrees. But when I concentrated the sun's rays on a tiny little point on the board, the temperature was raised by several hundred degrees.

This happens with us as individuals when we are able to increase and magnify the intensity of our lives upon one thing. When like Paul, we say, "This one thing I do," we have great power to accomplish that one thing.

Obviously, we can't think upon and magnify one thing all the time. But we can magnify a very few, and focus our attention on those important things one at a time.

Now you may think, "Well, I don't want to be that narrow." Obviously, you don't have to do anything. But remember, if I wanted to get my initials burned on that piece of wood, I couldn't do it without magnifying those sun rays by narrowing them down to one point. Now, I didn't have to put my initials on that piece of wood, but if that is what was important to me at the time, then I had to do it by focusing.

There is one thing of which we are absolutely certain. If we will focus our time, attention, ability, enthusiasm, and study on a few singular, worthwhile causes, we can multiply our power. If we choose to, we can multiply our income fivefold or tenfold—or even more (although, as we said before, the money shouldn't be our primary objective). Like the magnifying glass, focusing our energies can increase our effectiveness 100, 200, or even 300 percent. It is one of the most important keys to living successfully.

COMMITMENT

"Present your bodies a living and holy sacrifice,
acceptable to God."—Romans 12:1, NAS

Life has little zest if you aren't committed. It's important
to be committed—but to what? Be committed to those
things on which you are focusing—those short-range and
long-range objectives. Make a commitment to your goals.

As you know, we've made a commitment to God, our
families, our professions, and our health. It may sound
corny, but those four things have become our "magnificent
obsessions."

We have become obsessed with doing what we think
will glorify God. We're not all that sure what he intends
us to be. But by worshiping him, by trying to love our
neighbor as ourselves, by loving our wives as Christ loved
the church, and by bringing our children up in the discipline and instruction of the Lord, we feel we are fulfilling
our commitment to do what glorifies God. Seldom do we
talk to anyone seriously without talking to them about
God. Few days go by that we don't talk to someone about
Jesus Christ. We think it's important that everyone have
Jesus in their lives. We can't force him on anyone, and
we don't want to. God could have forced himself on them,
but he didn't, so why should we? But because of what
he has done for us, we must share.

It's also an obsession with us that we do the things that will benefit our families. And it's an obsession to build our professional abilities and take care of our health.

Now you may think, "I don't want to be obsessed." But we can assure you that if the things that are important to you don't become obsessions, you are not going very far.

We would rather die than not achieve our major goals. Now, there are many things that are slightly important to us but that we wouldn't die for. We're not stupid, and we're not going to die for a small cause—at least, not intentionally. But if giving our lives would glorify God, then we would be willing to do it. If somehow it would rescue our families, we would do it. If somehow it would further our professions, we'd think about it. (In this case, of course, the fourth priority doesn't really apply. Giving up our lives to maintain our health doesn't make sense!)

We haven't had to prove that we'd give up our lives for any of those things, but there are people who have. There are lots of people, for instance, who have given up their lives because they took a stand for God. Those people proved how important their faith was to them.

According to *Foxe's Book of Martyrs*, the apostle Peter was crucified with "his head being down and his feet upward," because he considered himself "unworthy to be crucified after the same form and manner as the Lord was." The apostle Paul was beheaded because of his devotion to the gospel of Jesus Christ. Through the centuries Christians have been fed to lions, burned at the stake, beheaded, and killed by other means because they remained faithful to Jesus Christ, who was tortured and put to death for them . . . and us.

BILL: There are also many instances of people who have given their lives for the sake of their families, or in the course of doing their jobs. During the Vietnam War, one of my close friends, Lt. Clebe McClary, was leading a patrol behind enemy lines. A hand grenade was thrown into a foxhole where ten of McClary's men were hiding. Immediately one of the men, a black sergeant, jumped on top of it with his own body. He was blown almost in half, but saved the lives of his nine buddies. I wouldn't want to do something like that unless I had to, but I think I would do it if it meant saving my family or friends.

Most of the time, of course, we don't have to concern ourselves with dying for our priorities. What's really important is that we *live* for them. Dying is a "split second" thing—it's over in an instant. But living must be done day after day—it's much harder. That's not to say that the actual situation of dying would be easy! But there is an important sense in which it is tougher to "hang in there" daily. Living for our priorities takes real commitment!

Whether or not we agree with all the things to which people commit themselves isn't the question. The fact remains that little is ever done by people who are only casually involved. The committed make things happen.

When we read about the accomplishments of a great man or woman, we frequently find that he or she had great difficulty to overcome. Mickey Mantle was one of the greatest baseball players in the history of the game. He played most of his career in pain. Wilma Rudolph won several gold medals as an Olympic sprinter. She was crippled as a child and not supposed to walk. O. J. Simpson is a football legend, but was also a cripple as a child. Glenn Cunningham had his legs horribly burned in a childhood accident, but he became a great miler. Were these not people with extraordinary commitment?

There was a time during the Second World War when England was backed into a corner and had virtually no defense. Across the English Channel, in France, Hitler was poised, ready to invade. Right at this time, Winston Churchill, the prime minister, spoke on the radio to all of England. What could he say? It looked as if they would be destroyed at any moment. Though a lot of British soldiers had gotten out of Dunkirk alive, they had no equipment and no weapons. Britain was virtually helpless.

But as the British people listened to Churchill on the radio, they were amazed to hear him conclude his speech with stirring words of commitment: "Victory, victory, victory at any price." This must be the attitude of the winner.

He or she must be one who thinks only of victory. The worse the situation becomes, the more completely he or she concentrates on victory.

BILL: I remember telling that story about Winston Churchill to one of my teammates back when I was playing football for the Cleveland Browns. He was a defensive back by the name of Larry Kellerman—small for a pro football player, but a tough, hardnosed, determined player. I told him the Churchill story about a week before a very important game, and he adopted Churchill's words as his motto for that game. All week long during practice he repeated over and over to himself, "Victory, victory, victory at any price." He saw himself as being like Churchill—determined to conquer regardless of the odds, regardless of what was against him.

When game time came, that phrase of Churchill's became Larry's and my private battle cry. He was the defensive right halfback and I was the defensive right end; this meant we played on the same side of the field and were together on tackles. So every time we made a tackle we would look at each other and shout, "Victory, victory, victory at any price." This might sound a little corny, but it was amazing how effectively we played during that game.

Out of Montgomery, Alabama, during the late 1950s comes another story of dedication and commitment. In Alabama at that time, blacks were expected to ride in the back of public buses. But on December 1, 1955, a black woman named Rosa Parks decided she didn't want to sit in the back of the bus. The bus driver tried to force her to move to the back, but she refused.

That was the beginning of an event that was pivotal in the U.S. civil rights movement. The blacks in Montgomery decided to stage a boycott of the bus system, and a young preacher named Martin Luther King, Jr., became its leader. A lot happened during that boycott. Quite a few blacks went to jail. Many were sprayed with high-pressure fire hoses or bitten by police dogs. Many faced guns and angry crowds. But they eventually succeeded in what they were trying to do. In December of 1956 the

Supreme Court ruled that segregation on public buses
is unconstitutional.

Now, whether or not you agree with the cause those
blacks were fighting for is beside the point. What is important is that they proved their commitment. What they
did was dangerous, and some of them even died. More
than a decade later, Martin Luther King himself made
the ultimate sacrifice for the same cause.

WINNERS MUST HAVE COMMITMENT

People who are winners are people who are committed.
They are obsessed with their goals. And they are willing
to make sacrifices to achieve those goals.

Do you know what is required of a person who wants
to become a doctor? People who have that goal must decide
in high school to study medicine. They have to have a
high IQ, but they also need a deep commitment. They
must make good grades all through college—not just pass-
ing grades, but near the top of the class. And they have
to do that in tough courses. They must do a great deal
of lab work and study long hours. Then, when they finally
get into medical school, their days become eighteen or
twenty hours long. And those long, grueling days continue
throughout their residency program. Because of the long
hours involved, people who want to be doctors have to
give up almost everything else that's important to them
for several years. Have you ever worked eighteen to
twenty hours a day for several days in a row? You get
very tired and sleepy, and you get to thinking, "I don't
know if this is worth it." But that's the kind of sacrifice and commitment that is required if medicine is your
goal.

This same kind of commitment is required for any number of other causes. For example, read Theodore White's
The Making of a President, the story of how John F.
Kennedy came to office. The process started decades in
advance. Back in 1937, John Kennedy's father, Joseph
Kennedy, Sr., decided he wanted to be president, and he
wanted to run for the office in 1940. But that year President Franklin Roosevelt decided to run for an unprece-

dented third term, and this decision pretty well eliminated the possibility that Joseph, Sr., could run. Then, in 1944, World War II was raging, and most people didn't want to change presidents right in the middle of the war. So, President Roosevelt was elected for a fourth term.

At that point, Joseph Kennedy, Sr., changed his plan. He still wanted a president in the family, but rather than run for office himself he decided to concentrate on getting his oldest son, Joseph, Jr., elected. But to his dismay Joseph, Jr., was killed a few years later when the plane he was flying blew up over the English Channel.

Joseph Kennedy, Sr., then turned his attention to John, the next-oldest male. At that time John was a very young man, much too young to run for president, but his father determined that he was going to be president of the United States. The whole Kennedy family became involved in the project, devoting a tremendous amount of time and effort for nearly twenty years to get John Kennedy elected. They spent millions of dollars, traveled hundreds of thousands of miles, shook millions of hands, faced thousands of hostile people.

John Kennedy faced two really big obstacles in becoming president. First, he was young—younger than any elected president in history. (Teddy Roosevelt had been younger when he served as president, but he had come into office through the death of another president; he had not actually been elected.) Second, Kennedy was Catholic, and no Catholic had ever been president. These obstacles were defeated because of amazing concentration by the Kennedy family on the purpose of getting young John F. Kennedy elected.

The Kennedys proved their commitment to something that was important to them. They were obsessed, and their obsession paid off in terms of reaching their objective. The same thing was true of Richard Nixon. Like the Kennedys, he devoted his life to becoming president.

Now, we're not discussing the merits of either Kennedy or Nixon as presidents. We're not even saying that being president is a worthy objective. But one thing is certain from the stories of the two presidents. With commitment, what seems impossible can be achieved.

WHAT IT TAKES TO WIN

The stories of Kennedy and Nixon also illustrate two important facts about commitment. One is that sometimes it takes a long time to reach important goals. In many cases, commitment must be for the long haul.

JIM: A friend of mine, Aaron Meyers, started with Tom James in 1967. He made a commitment to stay with the company for five years, no matter how difficult or discouraging his job might become. He knew he could not properly evaluate the opportunity without a relatively long-term commitment. I believe this showed very good judgment on his part. Many people give up on the verge of success because they have not made a long-term commitment and are unwilling to persevere in trying to reach their goals.

A second important principle about commitment is that it involves attention to detail. One of the things that got Kennedy elected was his family's tireless attention to the details of a successful campaign: meeting people, working on a local level, keeping careful records, planning every step carefully.

Bill Massie, a Baylor University student who excels in all he does, expresses it this way: "You must be committed to doing all of the little things required to succeed." Bill's commitment to the "little things" enabled him to earn about $10,000 his first summer as a student salesman for the Southwestern Company.

DON'T GET OBSESSED WITH THE WRONG THINGS!

Because commitment demands so much of us, it is very important that what we are committed to is worthy of our commitment! It is possible to let meaningless things, or the wrong things, become our "magnificent obsession," and this can be a tragic waste of time and energy.

BILL: I once knew a man who became interested in guppies. Now, there's nothing wrong with that. But this man became absolutely preoccupied with guppies. They became an obsession with him: he bred them, fed them,

*read books about them. He didn't even care about tropi-
cal fish in general—only guppies. And he wasn't interested in just ordinary, everyday guppies; he wanted
special, elite guppies.*

*Guppies were all this man talked about; they were
his total interest. Needless to say, he became a real bore
about them! He was a fine, brilliant, loving man with
a great mind. But after a while his friends and family
started to feel ridiculous. After all, how much interest
can one sustain in an extended discussion of guppies?
Fortunately, after a few years my friend lost interest
in guppies, but not before he lost a lot of valuable time
being obsessed with a harmless but hopelessly trivial
occupation.*

A relationship with Christ can be vitally important in
keeping us from being obsessed with things that are unworthy of our long-term commitment. That is because
the Lord tends to bring us sharply back to reality. He
asks the piercing question, "Why would a man labor for
meat that perishes?" If "thieves break through and steal"
a thing, it can't have ultimate worth, so why value it so
highly? If a thing rots, it must not have great value when
compared to eternity. To be really worth commitment, a
goal should have some eternal value.

It is possible to become obsessed by fears. In extreme
cases these fears become phobias. But more often, they
simply distract from the object of the worthy obsession.
For some reason, negatives always seem to be remem-
bered more easily than positives. It's possible to fixate
on one negative, harsh experience and forget all the encouraging success experiences.

A lot of people get obsessed with rejection. When they
make a sales call and someone tells them no, they think,
"Oh, poor me. This guy turned me down. He must not
like me. What's wrong with me? This is a lousy place to
sell. Nobody likes to buy."

*BILL: As a pro footballer, I used to retire every Mon-
day after we lost. But by Tuesday, I was zeroed in on
beating the next team. When you get too obsessed with
the rejection, you'll have problems. I guarantee that
people are going to criticize you if you do anything.*

If you do anything worthwhile, it's inevitable that you are going to face negative people.

JIM: The way I react to unjust criticism is, "Thank you. I appreciate that compliment." Now, I don't say it out loud, because it would sound sarcastic. But I say it to myself when they criticize me, because it reminds me that I'm doing something. In some cases, I take criticism as instruction, as evidence that I need to change something. But I try never to take criticism personally, because doing that could ruin me. I'd have to quit! That would be becoming obsessed with myself rather than with my objective. If I believe what I am doing is right, then I don't care too much what other people think. Why should I?

We have seen many people who had ability and potential fail because they became obsessed with problems—and especially because they became obsessed with themselves. One of the most talented salesman we have ever known is a failure at age fifty because he was obsessed with getting rich quick. (As we mentioned in the last chapter, an obsession with money is usually a form of obsession with oneself.)

There are many reasons for people's becoming obsessed with themselves. And the consequences can be awful. One lady we know shot herself to death—and she was only forty-five! She had several fine children and a couple of grandchildren. We don't know all her problems, but we can guarantee that we know her main problem. She thought about herself all the time. She had had several unfortunate things happen to her, but those same things have happened to many people who are now better people for having gone through them. This woman's suicide was caused not by her misfortunes, but by her preoccupation with herself. She turned all her time and attention inward.

KEEP YOUR COMMITMENT HIGH!

We have found that frequently reviewing what we've written about why our goals are important to us helps reinforce our commitment to those goals. Our commitments tend to be only as strong as our awareness of why we set our goals in the first place. That is one reason it is so important that our commitments be to worthwhile and meaningful goals.

What is commitment? We would say commitment is a blend of courage, desire, and determination, mixed with perseverance and guts. Commitment is a deliberate choice to never give up.

Ordinary people with extraordinary commitment achieve extraordinary results. Great achievers are people just like you who make a commitment to their goal.

Your commitment must be something much bigger than yourself. It must be outside yourself. Your obsession must be your cause—that which gives your life meaning and purpose. Let that be your magnificent obsession.

PREPARATION

"Be diligent to present yourself approved to God as a workman who does not need to be ashamed."—2 Timothy 2:15, NAS

One of the most important things we discovered as we searched for the things successful people have in common is preparation. Unfortunately, it's the one thing most of us would like to leave out! We'd like to tell you that preparation isn't necessary and that you can skip it, but you can't! It's a must, and it isn't easy. Successful people are few in number because the door is jammed with all kinds of barriers. And lack of preparation is among the most stubborn of barriers.

Racehorse Haynes, the famous trial lawyer, has an amazing record of success. The papers are full of colorful accounts of his ability to sway a judge and jury with his speaking skills. But there are many lawyers who can do an even better job in this area. What makes Haynes one of the best in the business is his meticulous preparation! He is especially adept at questioning the jurors, the people who are going to decide the merits of the case. He has an uncanny ability to screen out jurors who are likely to be hostile to his side or would likely render a guilty verdict on someone he's defending. He is a real student of human nature, and he chooses jurors who are going to vote his way. He has all kinds of reports made on prospective jurors. And he is also able to get a profile of a juror's personality simply by asking the right questions.

A POLITICAL SUCCESS STORY

In the last chapter we referred to Theodore White's book, *The Making of a President*, which tells the story behind the election that put John F. Kennedy in office. We stressed the Kennedy family's commitment to seeing that John Kennedy became president. But we also had to be impressed with the fantastic preparation the Kennedys made for that campaign. They pretty well infiltrated every precinct all over the country with their people.

You know how precinct politics work. Each party holds a precinct meeting at election time, and delegates are selected to go to a county meeting. At those county meetings people are chosen to go to the state convention, where still another group of delegates is selected to go to the national convention. Finally, at the national convention, the party's candidates are selected. By rounding up people who were favorable in most precincts, the Kennedys were able to dominate the democratic precinct meetings. By controlling the precincts, they were able to send delegates first to the county and the state meetings, and finally to the national conventions.

Never before had any presidential candidate organized a campaign so carefully at a local level. Had John F. Kennedy and his family not done all that complete preparation, there would have been no way he could have been the candidate in 1960. As we mentioned before, his youth and his Catholicism were two political strikes against him, and they normally would have kept him from being the Democratic candidate. But because the family went to such great lengths to prepare, Kennedy did become first the Democratic candidate and then president of the United States.

THE COWBOYS—ANOTHER SUCCESS STORY

The Dallas Cowboys football team started in 1960. By 1966, they had made it to the playoffs for the first time.

And only one time since then have the Dallas Cowboys failed to make it to the playoffs. They've made it to the Super Bowl more times than any other team. That's the best record in professional football. And one of the secrets behind this fantastic record is preparation. The thoroughness with which they prepare sets them apart from every other organization in football.

The Cowboys' system for scouting has been so successful that it has been almost universally adopted among pro teams. Again, their secret is preparation. They compile all kinds of records and information about the intelligence, speed, size, and aptitude of almost every college player in America, and they *computerize* the information. They also cultivate college coaches to promote a favorable attitude toward the Cowboys.

The draft should cause the Cowboys trouble because the teams with the best record pick last. Regardless, the Cowboys have still come up with good players. They get the best out of their turns in the draft because they do their homework.

One thing that continually amazes students of the NFL is the way the Cowboys keep coming up with great free agents. One more time, the secret is preparation. They study college talent. They know which players are going to be overlooked—the ones from obscure colleges, those sidelined by injuries that kept them out of the headlines, those who are just late bloomers.

The preparation the Cowboys make for each game is fantastic. They were the first to do computer printouts about what the other team is likely to do in every situation. Say, for example, that they are facing the St. Louis Cardinals, that there are three-and-a-half minutes left in the third period, that the Cardinals are trailing by six points and are on their own thirty-yard line, and that it's second down. The computer printout tells the Cowboys just what the Cardinals are likely to do in that situation. That way the Cowboys can be ready! Tom Landry has all these computer printouts on the sidelines giving him information based on probabilities discovered from the study of these teams.

One of the key reasons the Cowboys are winners is

that they are the best-prepared team in football. You can't
be a consistent winner without preparation.

How Should You Prepare?

One of the most important aspects of good preparation
is gathering the information you need to reach your goals.
Whatever your field, the written word can be an excellent
source of information. We recommend that you read inces-
santly—books, journals, magazines, whatever provides
the kind of information you need. The city library is filled
with materials that can enable you to become an expert
in the areas of your interest.

Another great source of information is other people.
It's smart to spend a lot of time questioning successful
men and women, asking for their ideas and input. Sometimes other people can be a valuable source of information
and guidance you simply can't find in books.

To get the most out of what you read or find out from
other people, try to get in the habit of asking yourself
questions about the information you are receiving. Ask
yourself this question about everything you read and hear:
"What does this book or person *really* mean to say?"
This will give you a much better understanding of the
book or the person than simply reading or listening would.
It's hard to transfer information from one mind to another
because every person's experience is so different. You can
transfer some information, but there really isn't a meaningful exchange of ideas until you ask yourself, "What
does this mean?" After that first question, ask other questions: "Why is this information important to me?" "How
can I use it?" And always *answer* your own questions.
If you get in the habit of doing this, you will always be
extremely well prepared.

It is important that you *apply* what you learn *as you
learn it.* Don't wait until you know everything before
you start using what you have learned. When you learn
something new, put it into practice immediately. If you
do not begin to use the new information within twenty-
four hours, you probably never will use it.

An important aspect of preparation is making lists of

ways to achieve your goals. As we mentioned earlier in
this book, we list three questions on each "goal sheet"
in our notebooks:

"What Is My Goal?"

"Why Is This Goal Important to Me?"

"How Can I Achieve This Goal?"

Part of our preparation is to sit down and write as many
ways as we can think of to achieve the goal. In quite a
few cases we may have to do a lot of study and research
to find the ways to achieve the goal. One of the best ways
to prepare is to seek the advice of those who may have
already achieved the goal you are striving to achieve.

PRACTICE PAYS OFF

Practice is another important part of preparation. Great
speakers practice their speeches. Great actors practice
saying their lines. Great athletic teams practice their
plays.

Brooks Robinson was one of the greatest third basemen
in baseball history. As a youngster, he began the practice
of having a hundred ground balls hit to him each day.
And he continued this practice through more than twenty
years of professional baseball. Is it any wonder that he
became a great infielder?

Was it natural talent or practice that made Mickey Mantle a great hitter? In his book, *Winners Never Quit*, Phil
Pepe says, "By the time he [Mickey Mantle] was five,
he was learning to be a switch-hitter! His dad would throw
right-handed while Mickey batted left, and his grandfather
would throw left-handed while Mickey batted right."

When Billy Graham first started in the ministry, he
preached his sermons to trees in the swamps of Florida.
He didn't share those sermons with people until they were
well prepared through endless practice.

Great salesmen practice their sales presentation until it becomes totally natural. If you want to excel . . .
practice!

BECOME AN AUTHORITY

It has been said that if a person would study thirty minutes every day on one specific subject for ten years, that person would be the world's foremost expert on that subject. At first, that sounds far-fetched, but think about it! Thirty minutes a day for five days comes to about two-and-one-half hours a week. If you do that for fifty weeks, you will have studied 125 hours in a year and 1,250 hours in ten years. If you read thirty pages an hour, you will have read 1,250 hours times thirty pages, or about 37,500 pages. If a typical book is about 200 pages long, that's about 185 books you would have read. I guarantee that anybody who has read 185 books on one subject knows a lot about that subject! He may even be called a leading authority.

What's the most complicated subject you can think of? How about brain surgery? Suppose you had read 37,500 pages of information relating to brain surgery. Don't you think you would know a lot about it? What could you *not* have found out that there is to know? You would know all about brain surgery—or at least all the book knowledge.

Suppose you also had been practicing what you were reading. Maybe you haven't actually operated on someone's brain, but you have observed for a certain number of hours. You have held the instruments and assisted in the operating room. Then after a few months you were allowed to move up close to the surgeon, helping with the actual surgery. You would have been closely involved in the actual process. If you had seen brain surgery done dozens or even hundreds of times, in addition to having read all that information, you could probably do a pretty good job of it yourself.

Being a good parent or teacher or salesman can be as complicated as being a brain surgeon. Since the surgeon is opening up a brain, and a parent, teacher, or salesman is opening up a mind, there is less difference than you would think. In fact, in some ways parenting, teaching, and selling are even more complicated than brain surgery. But most parents, teachers, and salesmen don't even think of putting in the kind of preparation time that a brain surgeon does.

No matter what your profession, there is no reason why you shouldn't be just as prepared as the most famous brain surgeon in the nation. Granted, if the surgeon isn't properly prepared, his patient could die, and your lack of preparation probably wouldn't result in someone's death. But something dies inside of you when you kill your own potential through lack of preparation.

PREPARATION MEANS SUCCESS

The people who are best prepared are usually going to be the ones who are most successful. In almost any field, the person who knows the most has astounding success. Do you know anyone who is the world's foremost authority on any subject who isn't extremely well paid—not only in terms of money, but usually in terms of personal satisfaction, too? And people become authorities through a lot of study and a lot of preparation.

JIM: I can honestly say that I decided I would become the world's foremost authority, or at least one of the world's foremost authorities, on building a business that sells custom clothing. But I didn't want to take ten years to become that much of an expert; I wanted to do it in five. So I studied an hour instead of thirty minutes a day. Now I feel, in all humility, that I am one of the world's foremost experts on how to successfully sell custom clothing. That is because I have prepared diligently—mostly by reading a great deal!

As my role in the company has changed, what I read has changed a little. While I was selling to my own clientele, what I read most were things that directly related to selling or directly related to my product. When my role changed to sales management, my study changed. I didn't stop reading about selling or about the product, but in addition I started studying some other things that were directly related to what I was doing as a manager. As my role changed to directing the company as a whole, I had to start studying still other things, like the importance of making a profit, or the way to keep expenses down.

Preparation pays. I guarantee if you will spend a definite period of time every day—thirty minutes, forty minutes, or an hour—on things that relate to your business, and if you will put into practice what you are studying, within five to ten years you will be either the world's foremost authority, or one of the foremost authorities, in your entire industry. And I guarantee that you will be one of the highest-paid people in your business.

You don't have to worry about there being too many other people who get a headstart on you. There is enough room for several world's-foremost-authorities, and enough money for all of them to make good pay. You are still going to do great!

There is a tendency to say that those who excel have "natural ability." A careful study, however, will find that those who excel, are those who "set goals, make commitments to their goals, prepare thoroughly to achieve their goals, and do goal-oriented work." (We'll talk about goal-oriented work in the next chapter.)

One final word: Beware of lopsided preparation! Any diet will work, but the best ones are well balanced. If all your work is in your business, it's no good. You should also give time to reading about improving your relationship to God and your family. The Bible is tough to beat in both areas! There are other books to be read in both areas, as well. Again, it is crucial to apply whatever you read. Successful people are those who make a habit of doing all the things that failures don't do. One thing that successful people do is make a habit of careful preparation.

FOR NEW IDEAS

What does it mean?

Why is it important to me?

How can I use it?

GOAL-ORIENTED WORK

"But seek first His kingdom and His righteousness; and all these things shall be added to you."—Matthew 6:33, NAS

"Show me a man who works hard, and I'll show you a success." That's an inspiring statement. The trouble is, it's just not necessarily true! We know a lot of people who work very hard and yet never make it. And there are others who seem to work less, yet accomplish important objectives.

Hard work *is* a vital ingredient of success—but not just any hard work. To be a winner, you need to do the *right kind of work*—the kind that we like to call "GO work." What do we mean by GO work? The letters stand for "goal-oriented." Goal-oriented work is whatever moves you toward your objectives.

Now, there is a lot of work you can do that won't help you do that. In fact, there is a lot you can do that will get in the way of your achieving your goals. It is a well-accepted principle that any work you do will expand to fill the time alloted for it. But that work might very well be nothing more than paper shuffling. It may not be bad in itself. But while you're doing "non-GO" work, you can't be doing "GO" work. That's why you need to examine

the things you do and determine whether they help move
you toward your goals or not.

If you want to be successful, you should seldom let
yourself get in a situation that is totally non-GO. The
apostle Paul understood this principle; his entire life was
a powerful example of GO work. Put him before a king,
and he would tell of his Damascus Road experience. Put
him in prison, and he would win the jailer to faith in Christ.
Allow him to be bitten by a snake, and he would make
even that situation GO for God!

It is obvious that Paul was one of the most GO men
who ever lived. And his example may be hard to follow
to the letter. But we honestly believe that a modern, well-
rounded, committed person will find that most circumstances of life can be GO!

*BILL: This doesn't mean that we should never relax!
If we never do any activities of the tension-relieving
type, we could develop health problems from stress. But
there are plenty of activities that are both tension relieving and goal achieving. I find that jogging relieves a
lot of my tension. I can jog four or five miles and my
stress is gone. But jogging also helps me in achieving
weight control and cardiovascular (heart) fitness. Both
are physical goals of mine.*

*One of my most important goals is to love my wife
as Christ loved the church. His love for the church was
sacrificial and unconditional, and it took him to the
cross (Acts 20:28). But in my case that kind of love could
also take me to a nice restaurant with my wife, if that's
what she likes. And even that tension-releasing experience is also a GO activity, because it moves me toward
the objective of loving my wife.*

*A dinner like that becomes less GO if it is used for
small talk, rather than for learning where she's hurting
and how I can better meet her needs. It can be counter-
or non-GO if there is conflict, selfishness, jealousy, com-
petition, or trivial discussion.*

When we start thinking in terms of GO and non-GO
activities, we start seeing life in a different perspective.
For instance, we have come to the conclusion that television is non-GO for us. Even when we watch with our wives

and families, there is little interaction among us. TV teaches little that will help us love God more or improve us professionally. And it is counter-GO in a physical sense because we usually end up snacking and we use no muscles except those on which we sit.

One of the problems with drugs and alcohol is that they are basically counter-GO. They stop the maturing process; if you get into drugs at age thirteen and finally kick the habit at twenty-one, then you will still be thirteen emotionally. And drugs and alcohol interfere with motivation. This in turn can make GO work seem unattractive. It gets harder and harder for the person on drugs or the alcoholic to work toward worthwhile, meaningful goals.

JIM: Since I'm a salesman (and everyone is in sales to some degree), let's look briefly at how GO work relates to sales. Suppose I work hard to come up with several hundred names, addresses, and phone numbers of prospective clients. Then say I am very diligent in calling all of those people. I do such a great job of making phone calls for appointments that I get some uninterrupted time with every single one of them. Then I go out on the first call and make the greatest sales presentation I've ever given. To the next prospect, I give one that is just a little better—not only the greatest I've ever given but the best that person has ever heard.

All this hard work is great and should earn me a lot of sales—if I'm calling on people who have enough money to buy my product! Even if I do many things right—I locate lots of prospects, line up many appointments, and give excellent sales presentations—if I try to sell to the wrong people I'm not working smart. And all my work is non-GO work.

Remember, GO work is work that will help you achieve your goals. If your goal is selling, that means calling on the people who might want to buy your product. Let's suppose you are selling television sets. Would you want to call on blind people? Probably not. Or if you were selling radios, would you want to call on deaf people? If you were selling big tractors, would you call on apartment dwellers? Trying to do those things would be absolutely absurd! There might be a blind person

*somewhere who wants a television, or an apartment
dweller somewhere who owns a big farm and will buy
several tractors, but basically, the whole concept is ridiculous!*

*GO work in sales means doing everything you can
to help your customers discover all the good reasons
for buying and to overcome what they see as reasons
for not buying. You can't persuade them to buy something they don't want or need. If Randy White was a
salesman, he might be able to do that, because he's one
of the strongest men in football. He might sell through
intimidation, but I can't, and you probably can't,
either.*

THE GO WORK LIST

Limiting our activities to GO work is part of the entire
system for success we have been discussing. In order to
do GO work, you first have to know what your goals are.
This means starting from the beginning and writing out
your goals—choosing the objectives on which to focus
your energy, effort, ambition, and enthusiasm. Second,
you have to make a commitment to yourself and to your
project. Third, you might have to go back and spend some
time in preparation.

Then, when you've done all those things, you're ready
to get started doing the actual work on reaching your
goals. But even then there's some more writing to do.
Before you actually start to do GO work, it's smart to
make lists of activities that would be GO for every one
of your major objectives. If you don't do this, going
through the day will be like going through a grocery store
without a shopping list. Whatever you see as you walk
down the aisles attracts your attention. If you simply pick
up what catches your eye at a grocery store, you will
probably end up buying things you don't need. Then, when
you get home, you might find that you didn't buy something you needed desperately.

If you make a list before you go to the grocery store,
then you're far more likely to buy the things you need
and avoid buying the things you don't need. And the same

thing is true with GO work. Making a list of GO activities for each goal will help you concentrate on doing the GO work and avoid wasting time on activities that aren't GO.

Now, the idea of making a list seems so simple that many people say, "You know, I don't need to do that." But then these people are never able to focus in on doing the things they need to do to succeed!

It's important to make such lists of GO activities in order to accomplish each of your important goals. If you don't make lists, you will tend to get distracted by trivial activities. You will forget what activities are GO. You just can't keep everything concerning your goals in your head; the lists function as reminders.

When making your list, don't just put down anything and everything that comes to mind. Include only what is GO work—activities that help you achieve your objectives. It's very important that these lists be thorough and specific. As we said in the first chapter, even the best architect demands a detailed blueprint to construct a building. He doesn't just wing it. We have been amazed to discover that most people "wing it" in the most important areas of life—their relationship with God, their family life, and their profession.

A calendar or an appointment book is essential for people who want to achieve a lot through GO work. After you compile your list of GO activities, you need to put them on your calendar; otherwise, mundane activities will tend to occupy your time. We schedule important GO activities weeks or months in advance. In some cases we plan a year or two ahead.

What Should Be on Your List?

We can't tell you exactly what should be on your GO work list. It depends on your goals. If you are a student, your list would include attending all classes, listening carefully, and taking good notes. It would include a definite study schedule.

If you are a Sunday school teacher, your list would include study, lesson preparation, prayer, and visitation.

JIM: In the first chapter I mentioned Ash Deshmukh,

*who is one of the most successful clothing salesmen in
the country. Ash has a list of twenty GO activities that
he has compiled for his job. He is diligent in working
his list. And doing this has paid off for him.*

Bob Sherrer is a successful Christian, husband, father,
Sunday school teacher, and division president. One of
Bob's secrets is thorough preparation and confining his
activity to the essential. You won't find Bob doing tension-
relieving busy work. Bob's activities are a genuine reflec-
tion of his values.

*BILL: One of my goals is to be physically fit. What
is GO work relating to this goal? Here is my list:*

GO Work—Physical

1. *Yearly physical at Cooper Clinic [the best preventive
   medicine, cardiovascular clinic in the world].*
2. *Run four miles, four days per week, and do fifty sit-
   ups on nonrunning days. [A four-mile jog is just about
   right for me. Of course, this specific goal could vary.
   You might prefer to walk or to bicycle. But it is important to set specific goals.]*
3. *Eliminate salt, sugar, chicken fat, and nondairy cream-
   ers from my diet. [My triglycerides are a little high,
   so I have to watch these foods.]*
4. *Restrict starch, animal fat, and other fattening foods.
   [This relates to my goal of weight control.]*
5. *Weigh 240 pounds, keep heart rate at fifty beats per minute, and avoid non-GO stress.*

As we have mentioned, loving God is number one on
our list of goals. It is therefore GO for us to spend a
significant amount of time alone with God. Some would
say that is a waste of time—or, worse, a complete delusion.
But we know that since we love him we'd like to spend
time in reading his Word, in prayer, and in worship. Doing
this gives us perspective. It's tough to live a trivial life
when we constantly check in with the Creator of the universe. And much of our stress is drained off because he
helps us see what is really important.

Not all religious activity is GO, however, if your goal
is eternal life and a relationship with God. You can do

good works, go to church, give generously, and read the Bible, but if you do not know Jesus Christ as Savior you do not have life and have no hope of heaven. When it comes to the goal of knowing God and putting him first in your life, the most important GO action is to admit your sin to God, repent (turn away from your sin), and invite Jesus Christ into your life. Until you are willing to repent and believe, all religious activity is non-GO. But once you surrender yourself in faith to Christ, you are born again. And then it becomes GO to grow through Bible study, prayer, and Christian fellowship. Then GO work means loving all people with "agape" love. It means loving your neighbor and yourself and, above all, God. It means being filled with the Spirit and sharing your faith with others by your life and witness.

Now Comes the Hard Work!

Making lists of GO work and putting the work on your calendar are great ways to start. But obviously you can't stop there. You have to actually *do* what is on the list. And that's where the hard work comes in! Everything costs something, doesn't it? If you are going to do really well in life, you have to pay the price. And, again, it's foolish to pay a big price in terms of work that isn't goal oriented.

Albert Gray, in his speech, "The Common Denominator of Success," says, "Successful people have formed the habit of doing the things that failures don't like to do." That's another way of saying that winners are willing to pay the price for success by forming the habits that will enable them to achieve their goals. Sometimes that means doing things the hard way! And it almost always involves hard work. Failures are always seeking pleasing methods while successful people seek pleasing results.

JIM: The most pleasing method I could think of for selling would be to drive through town and honk, and have people come out and say, "I'll buy two; I'll buy three; I'll buy. . . !" I mean, that would really be fun! Or maybe it would be just as pleasant to just sit in an office with my feet propped up on a desk and have

people come in one after the other to buy my products.
That would be a pleasing method with pleasing results.
But the two virtually never go together. There is usually
a price of GO work to be paid to get good results!

We have heard of a few accomplishments that were
accidents. But even those accidents took place while someone was trying to accomplish something. For instance,
many years ago there was a scientist who created a concoc-
tion that was a type of glue. He dropped the bottle in
which he was keeping the solution, and it hit the cement
floor. But the glass didn't fly everywhere. The formula
was very sticky and it stuck to the glass. Even though
the bottle broke it didn't shatter.

The scientist thought, "That must be useful," so he
set to work trying to figure out a use for his formula.
He came up with the idea of using it in car windshields.
He stuck two pieces of windshield glass together with
this glue, so that if someone broke the windshield, the
glass wouldn't fly everywhere.

The result was what we call safety glass! It's discovery
was more or less an accident. But that accident wouldn't
have happened had the inventor not been working toward
a goal.

BILL: If you want to win in football, you have to
get in shape. Training camp is tough. The body aches
from two grueling months of two hard workouts a day.
The hours are long and the workouts rugged. The play-
ers end up bruised from head to toe—taxed to the limit.
It is not a pleasing method, but necessary for pleasing
results.

My most vivid memories of twelve years of pro football
were of those twenty-four months of training camp (two
months per year). I really didn't look forward to that
torture, but I must admit that much of my individual
success and my success as a part of the team was due
to that tough work. With the soreness and bruises came
the realization that what I was doing was absolutely
GO.

If you succeed, it won't be because you have settled
for pleasing methods. It will be because you have been
willing to pay the price by doing the things that failures

don't like to do. If you don't know what results you want, you aren't going to pay the price. If you don't make a strong, powerful commitment, you are going to quit. If you aren't well prepared, you are going to experience so many failures and frustrations that you won't continue to get back up after being decked! But if you don't work hard, you just won't get where you want to go.

How to Get Pleasing Results

JIM: If you are in sales, one of the toughest things to overcome is "call reluctance." For some reason, you resist contacting the customers, but to get results you must make the calls.

Work should be fun. If you'll try to figure out how every call you make can be fun and exciting for the prospect, I guarantee that you are going to have fun, too. I try to do something that's going to make my presentation just a little bit different and more fun, so my client will be glad I came and glad to have me come back.

When I was searching for the keys to success I would ask the customers I called on, "What enabled you to be so successful? How did you become one of the leaders in your field?" I was seriously interested. It was not just a technique. But I soon found that the people I asked liked to talk about themselves, and my questions helped make my call fun for them.

If you have done something well and someone asks you about it, don't you get excited telling them how you did it? Everyone is like that. I can't remember an occasion when questioning someone about his success failed to capture his interest!

Now, if you try to do this without having any genuine interest in the customer, it won't work. He will recognize it just as a gimmick, and he'll resent it. But if you are genuinely interested in what he has to say, you can find something in his office about which you can ask. Since it's displayed, he probably is interested in it. And he'll enjoy telling you about it.

I've found that it's usually not good to ask about

*the customer's wife and children. It's too obvious a
maneuver, and he'll see through it. Everybody says
things like, "Your children are beautiful." Compli-
menting family will work only if you know something
specific about them and can comment on it genuinely:
"Your son sure does look like his Dad."*

*Many times a customer will have something in his
office that indicates an accomplishment about which
you can ask.*

*Once I called on an attorney who was a former Uni-
versity of Texas football player. I didn't know anything
about his background, but I soon began to get strong
hints. On his floor he had a little throw rug made of
green astroturf, with yard markers and goal lines and
the initials UT in orange. So I said, "I've never seen
a rug like that before! Did you go to the University of
Texas?" "Yeah, I did," he answered. "Did you play football there?" He proceeded to tell me about his University
of Texas days and about playing football. That attorney
really had fun telling me those stories. I listened with
both ears and both eyes; I wasn't saying to myself, "I
wish he would hurry up and get through." And after
a few minutes of talking, he said, "I know you didn't
come here just to hear about my football, and I do need
some clothes. So, let me see what you've got." This experience convinced me that my being a good listener about
something my customer enjoyed telling me had opened
him up to me. I sold a ton . . . but not more than he
wanted to buy.*

*This principle of being an open-minded listener
doesn't just apply to sales. It's the same in almost any
endeavor. Ask about something that person likes to discuss, and then listen carefully. Find an area of common
interest. That opens the door for you!*

*Do all you can to make your transactions fun for
the other person. I guarantee that if it's fun for him,
it's going to be fun for you.*

*I'm not talking about telling jokes all the time. There
are some people who can do that and it may help, but
most people aren't good at telling jokes. What I'm sug-
gesting you do is to be sure that what you are doing*

is GO work—and have at it! You are going to do so well that you will not believe it yourself. You are going to be so happy and pleased. And the reason you'll be having such a ball is that you'll know you are accomplishing what you wanted to accomplish. That is the most pleasing result possible.

AFFIRMATIONS

"Do nothing from selfishness or empty conceit, but with humility of mind let each of you regard one another as more important than himself."—Philippians 2:3, NAS

JIM: In 1965, I went to work for Spencer Hays, who was then a Southwestern Company sales manager and now is the chairman of the executive committee of Tom James Company. That was the year before Tom James was opened.

When I first started working with Spencer, I admired him tremendously, but I must admit I thought he was a little peculiar at first, because he was always saying to himself things like, "My job is to add joy and happiness to the lives of everyone I meet today." And he would try to get me to do the same thing. He would urge me to remind myself over and over to "be service-minded." He would suggest that I remind myself repeatedly to "think in the interest of others, rather than in my own interest." Spencer tried to get me to say, "I can! I will! I am going to do it!"

Finally I began to understand what Spencer was doing, and what he was trying to get me to do. He was affirming that which he wanted to achieve. He was reminding himself over and over of that which was impor

tant to him. And as he affirmed those things that were important to him, he was also renewing his commitment to them. The words Spencer spoke to himself focused his time, energy, efforts, and thoughts on the task at hand. They brought back into his mind the picture of that which he was trying to achieve. And they helped keep him emotionally involved with his goals and objectives.

Once I understood the value of the verbal affirmations Spencer was making, I decided to try making some myself. My first real application of what Spencer was teaching me was to set a goal: "I will be the kind of man I can respect." I wrote the goal out on a 3 x 5 card. Then I gave Spencer a copy of this card and asked him to remind me if he ever saw me acting in a manner that was inconsistent with my goal. But, more importantly, I carried the original card around in my shirt pocket, and I made a point of reading the card several times during every day.

Whenever I would read that card, certain pictures would come to mind. I would see myself acting in ways that were consistent with my goal. I would imagine myself doing things that were pleasing to God, being a good husband and a loving father, working diligently. Those pictures reminded me what my goal was, and what it involved. They also created in me an emotional response that continued to strengthen my commitment to my goal. Soon I realized that making my regular affirmations was helping me move toward my goal.

As time went on I added other 3 x 5 cards with other goals written on them. Some were:

My goal is to love God with all my heart and all my soul and all my mind.

My goal is to love Arlene [my wife] as Christ loves the church.

My goal is to bring up my children in the instruction and discipline of the Lord.

My goal is to love my children and show them the attributes of the heavenly Father through my life.

My goal is to love my neighbor as myself.

My goal is to seek the kingdom of God and his righteousness.

My goal is to gain the Holy-Spirit-directed knowledge and application of the Bible.

My goal is to help build Tom James Company to a $100,-000,000 business.

My goal is to contribute to the lives of all of my associates.

My goal is to keep spiritual values above all that the world has to offer.

I have had many other written goals, but these are examples of some that have been important to me. And with every goal the process was the same. I would write the goal on a 3 x 5 card and read it several times each day. Doing this would immediately bring a mental picture into focus, and the picture would stir an emotional response. As I affirmed the importance of my goals, I would be spurred to learn and to take action . . . goal-oriented action.

Before I started learning about affirmations from Spencer I had done several things well, but never over a prolonged period of time. But the principle of affirmation he showed me gave me a way to keep my goals in focus and a way to constantly renew my commitment. I started being successful on a more consistent basis.

Needless to say, I thought Spencer was a genius! Then, as I started to read more and more in my field, I saw that most of Spencer's good ideas came from books. I started thinking that maybe Spencer was not so smart after all, because these concepts he was teaching were not original. But then I started noting something else. Books are available to everyone; many people read good books. But not everyone applies the ideas he gets from books. If there is genius in an idea, there is equal genius in application. Spencer Hays is a genius in the application of ideas. And one of the most valuable things he taught me was how to apply the principle of affirmation to the process of achieving goals.

The Power of Affirmation

What does it mean to affirm? To us, it means reading over our goals and positively asserting that these goals have meaning, that they are worth working to achieve. We affirm our goals in order to stay aware of them—to keep them in focus. And we affirm our goals to remind ourselves of the work that needs to be done to achieve them.

The practice of affirming goals works because words, pictures, and feelings can have a powerful effect upon us. They influence our attitudes. Zig Ziglar says, "Your attitude determines your altitude." Affirming our goals lets us use our own words and the pictures they bring to mind to influence our attitudes.

Like all people, we have a tendency to become self-centered. Paul E. Billheimer, in his book entitled *Destined for the Throne*, says, "The quintessence of all our mental and nervous disorders is over-occupation with personal ego; namely, self-centeredness. When the personality becomes centripetal, that is, ego-centered, it disintegrates. Out of extreme self-centeredness arises defensiveness, hostility, and aggressive antisocial behavior. . . . to make one's self his center is self-destruction." But the process of reading our goals and affirming them helps keep this from happening by helping us focus our attention outside ourselves—on to God, our families, our associates, or our responsibilities and opportunities. Without those 3 x 5 cards, we have a consistent tendency to forget those things that are most important.

Seeing Ourselves As God Sees Us

JIM: I also put Scripture verses and prayer reminders on some of my 3 x 5 affirmation cards. These cards remind me to think on the things of God. I list things for which I can praise God—all the attributes of God are praiseworthy. Praising God takes my focus off of self.

Back in 1955, while a freshman at Howard Payne College, I took a Bible course. In that class Dr. Nat

Tracy told us something to this effect: "No one will ever be all he can be until he sees himself as God sees him." I have thought about what that means many times over the past twenty-nine years. God sees us as poor, hopeless, lost, and miserable—unworthy sinners in need of redemption. But God sent Jesus to die for us and to redeem us. And after we receive Jesus Christ as Savior and Lord, we become the children of God. Then God sees us as his children.

I now see myself as a child of God. And I frequently affirm that which God has done for me. I can affirm, "I feel healthy; I feel happy; I feel terrific," knowing that as a child of God I have good reason to feel healthy, happy, and terrific.

Of course, people can use affirmations to influence their attitudes in a positive manner whether or not they have received Jesus Christ. Humanism teaches techniques of "affirmation," but humanism can never bring anyone into a proper relationship with God. A proper relationship with God is worth working for, but we cannot earn it by working for it. Jesus Christ is the means to a proper relationship with God. We can use affirmations to remind us of what God has done for us, but we cannot affirm ourselves into a state of godliness.

Some writers write of the "infinite potential" of man. And it *is* amazing what man can achieve. However, we reject the concept of "man's infinite potential." The God of the Bible is infinite, but man is finite. Any ability a man has comes by the grace of God. Any man who does not receive eternal life through Jesus Christ is to be pitied, no matter what his human achievements may be.

We recognize that man is special among God's creatures; nevertheless, man is a created being. God is the Creator. Only the Lord God may be exalted. The Christian who is truly submissive to God has a much higher opinion of man than does the humanist, who in effect denies God and makes man answerable only to himself. The highest position that man can attain is at the point where he is totally submitted to the will of his Creator. Man cannot genuinely succeed solely through the affirmation of his own goals. Genuine success means knowing and doing the will of God.

WHY GOAL CARDS HELP

We use goal cards to remind ourselves every day, several times a day, what is really important. Maybe you're like we are. You've said to yourself, "Man, this is really important. I must remember it." Then, an hour or two later, you think, "What was it I was going to remember?" Some of those things you thought were important but didn't write down you've lost forever. You probably have it stored in your mind somewhere, but you just can't seem to retrieve it. Some things are just too important to depend on your memory.

Remember the story in chapter 3 about the magnifying glass? Failing to carry your goal cards and read them is like not having your magnifying glass when you need it. There might be plenty of sunshine and you might want to burn your initials on something, but if you don't have that magnifying glass you can't do it.

You can only achieve that upon which you focus your thoughts and efforts. What the cards do is to bring your attention back to your main purposes. Every time you bring your goals back into the center of your thinking, you are presented with an opportunity to recommit yourself to them. You are reminded of the importance of further preparing yourself to achieve them. You remember the GO work you planned to do to achieve them. So you are not only affirming your goals, but reminding yourself of the other components of success: commitment, preparation, and goal-oriented work.

JIM: One time I drove home from the airport after having been out of town for a week. Wearily I pulled into the driveway, only to find it blocked with bikes and other toys. My first reaction was to blow up. But one of my affirmations that day had been "to love my children and show them the attributes of the heavenly Father through my life." Remembering that got me back on track and helped me refuse to be trivial with my children. I decided to save my anger for more important things. So I moved the bikes, parked the car, and went into the house with a smile of greeting.

BILL: I remember coming into the kitchen one evening and reaching into the cabinet for a banana, but all the bananas were dark and rotten. My first impulse was anger—how many times had I told Mavis (my wife) about not letting bananas go bad? But I had just finished affirming my goal "to love my wife as Christ loves the church." That means unconditional love, and that kind of love makes bananas seem unimportant. So I found something else to eat, threw the bananas away, and said nothing about the incident to Mavis.

These two little irritating events gave us a perfect opportunity to make use of our affirmations concerning our children and our wives. Jim's affirmation reminded him that bikes improperly left out are not nearly so important as are loving family relationships. Bill's helped him keep in mind that three rotten bananas were not nearly so important as Mavis's beautiful smile and neat dress, and the excellent dinner she had prepared. Those affirmations played an important role in helping each of us move toward realizing one of our most important goals.

AFFIRMING FUTURE REALITIES

Some people have trouble with the idea of affirmations because most affirmations involve future reality. After all, you are affirming goals, and goals have to do with what is not yet accomplished. But this bothers people because they have been taught all their lives to "be realistic." They might say, "Well, I'm not a great success. If I affirm a really big goal for myself in business, won't that just be indulging in pipe dreams? Isn't it unrealistic to affirm situations that aren't present realities?"

But affirming future realities is part of the way the process works. When we read one of those 3 x 5 cards, the pictures that come to our minds are pictures of the future—of the way things will be when we achieve our goals. And it is partly the discrepancy between that visualized future and the reality of the present that spurs us on toward achieving our goals.

What happens is that affirming a really big goal makes us uncomfortable, because we know we fall short of the goal. Affirming something that is not presently true creates tension, and most of us don't like the pressure, so we look for a way to relieve the tension.

As we said earlier, there are two ways to do this. One is to actually start achieving the goal we have been affirming. The other is to give up the goal. Either way will work. But one way means we make progress and the other means we don't progress.

What most people haven't found out is that if they'll just accept the tension for a period of time, progress will occur. They will begin actually achieving their goals, and what they've been affirming will actually come true. Then the tension goes away. Unfortunately, most people get uptight and nervous when they first experience the tension that comes with affirming high goals. They want to quit reading the affirmations and forget their goals.

Now, we can't make anybody do anything. Each person has to choose for himself whether to keep affirming the goal and making progress toward it or to quit. But we think it's much smarter to accept the tension rather than to give up the goals.

The Bible has a lot to say about the process of affirming future realities. It calls this process "faith." Faith is that which you have prior to the reality. Hebrews 11:1 says, "Now faith is the substance of things hoped for . . ." What is the key word in that verse? Most people would say *faith*—or *substance* or *hope*. But we believe the key word is actually *is*. Faith *is* substance.

What this means is that God always provides *in advance*. In the Genesis account of creation we notice he created first the air and then the birds. He made water before he made fish and the Garden before he made man. If he had done it in reverse, the birds would have had no air in which to fly or to breathe. The fish would have had no water to swim in or no oxygen to breathe through their gills. Man would have had no Garden to supply shelter and food!

Christ died and rose again to provide forgiveness and life, and we accept it as a finished provision for our need. So when we feel the need for forgiveness, or life after death, or life in abundance now, we exercise faith. "Faith *is* substance." The provision has already been made! We act by faith and accept God's provision.

But even though God provides in advance, his provisions don't come to us until we begin to act in faith. Ten lepers came to Christ asking for healing. He told them to go to the priest and offer sacrifice. (The Law clearly commanded that no leper could mix with others until first he went to the priest and proved that he was totally cleansed.) So the men did what Jesus told them to, and the Bible says they were healed "as they went" (Luke 17:14). What a perfect example of the way faith works! The men were not healed until they started for the priest to show him they were healed. They actually "acted as if" they were healed before they were healed in reality. That's faith. It is affirming a thing that doesn't appear to be presently true, but that comes true when you begin to "act as if." Since the provision has already been made, it *is* reality!

BILL: Often people say to me, "Man, you have a lot of pressure on you. I don't see how you stay so loose and relaxed." Well, I don't think of it as pressure at all.

In pro football the pressure was often tremendous. But I played for twelve years, and I would have gone crazy if I hadn't learned to deal with stress.

One of the most important things I learned is that logic is ineffective against the emotion of anxiety. Emotions are responsive to action. Before a big game I could have rationalized, "You've been playing a long time. Why get nervous now?" But all the logic in the world would have failed! What I needed was action. Any football player will tell you that after the first contact in a game he is no longer unduly uptight.

Making use of affirmations has a similar effect on the emotions. It is a kind of action. When we affirm our goals we create a positive, powerful picture of ourselves achieving the goal. And that has a calming effect on us—it helps us get rid of stress.

Another discovery I made when I was a football player about handling pressure is that it is much better to attack any challenging task a little at a time. In foot-ball, that meant one play at a time. If you asked me, "Can you win the World's Championship?" I would have said, "Sure." But I would have probably felt over-whelmed and apprehensive about the prospect. If you had asked, "Can you play the trap?" I could have said "Sure" without any anxiety.

Doing any job is a snap in its component parts. Like someone said, "It's hard by the yard, but a cinch by the inch!" In high-pressure situations I simply picture myself accomplishing my goals one play at a time, be-cause I discovered when I was in pro football that that's the way you win the game.

The principle of taking any big job one step at a time works for making a speech, too. In City-Wide Crusades the crowd I face is often huge. In prisons I often speak to large and unruly audiences. The pressure could get to me, but I again break the job down into its simple parts and verbally and mentally affirm my ability to do each part—careful preparation, total familiarity with my material, concentration on my purpose, excite-ment about my subject, earnest prayer, and all the other things important to effective speaking! The best way I've ever discovered to fight pressure in any situation is to review written affirmations.

Every one of us is faced every day with the need to decide something about affirmations. As we touched on before, if we're affirming our goals properly, every one of them is going to involve a future reality. After all, why affirm something that has already been achieved?

If we're going to make progress, we're going to have to affirm the achievement prior to its realization. The dis-crepancy between the goal and the present situation will inevitably cause stress, so we have to choose that tempo-rary stress. But the stress is soon dissolved by the satis-faction of accomplishment. How long this process takes will depend on a number of factors: how clearly we have defined our goals, how strong our commitment is, how thoroughly we have prepared, and how hard and effec-tively we've worked.

The Mechanics of Making Affirmations

When you review your affirmations is up to you. When possible, it's best to do this while you're not doing anything else, because distractions at the time you're reading your affirmations could interfere with the clarity of your focus. But some people like to read their affirmations while they're shaving, or while they jog.

A good method is to put your goals on an audio cassette, so you can listen to your own voice reading your goals while you are driving or getting ready to go to bed. It's better than listening to the radio, because it is goal oriented.

BILL: In my book, Expect to Win, *I tell of an extremely interesting experience I had with this method of reviewing and affirming my goals:*

I became so convinced of the power of the mind that I engaged in a project that had monumental impact on my performance in football. I made tapes of little talks to myself, about seven minutes in length, on my recorder. The cassette sounded like this:

"Charge. Charge. Every time the word charge *floats through your mind, it will activate all the suggestions on this tape. Dominate your opponent. Dominate him. Fire across the line, overpower him. Feel his body crumble beneath your power. Throw him down on the inside, rush to the outside, and sack the quarterback. Pursue, pursue, pursue. Pursue until you hear the whistle. On running downs, destroy the blocker. Fire through the ball carrier. . . ."*

On and on the tape went for seven minutes, filled with powerful, positive suggestions concerning things I would accomplish during the game. I was convinced that this type of programming would promote mental pictures that would gravitate toward my playing in a super way. These suggestions would program my subconscious mind and during the game they would be "played back" when I said the word charge *to myself. "Charge!" would be the mental electrode that would trigger the powerful suggestions in the tape. So, I listened to that tape in the mornings several times on my way to work, before going to bed, and over and over again all week long prior to the game.*

But something went wrong. In the game, I played the most horrible football I've ever played in my life! In the film-study session the following Tuesday morning, the coaches were yelling and screaming at me, saying, "You hit an all-time low! You were terrible!"

After viewing the film of that particular game, I went out of the film-study session smiling. You might ask, "Why were you smiling after playing such a horrible game and getting chewed out by your coaches?" It had dawned on me in the study of the films that I was playing precisely in the way I had put the suggestions into my subconscious. I had said, "Charge. Charge," in a rather hypnotic tone, and the whole mood of the tape was in a monotone—almost as if I was just waltzing through my assignments. Sure enough, when game time came, I was waltzing through my assignments and gliding through my responsibilities in a sleepy manner. I knew if I could change the tone of the tapes, I would also be able to change the way I would perform in the game.

I went back to my room, and began to develop a new recording. This time the tape was literally shouting with emotion and power. "CHARGE! CHARGE! Every time the word charge explodes out of your mouth, it will activate all the suggestions on this tape! DOMINATE YOUR OPPONENT! DOMINATE HIM! . . ." It was done in explosive bursts of energy with great enthusiasm and shouting.

The next week, we played against St. Louis. All week long, I listened to the tapes of shouted commands many times every day, and finally I was on my way to the game with the team. I made a deal with myself that I would listen to the tape repeatedly until we arrived in St. Louis. We flew for about an hour and a half aboard a chartered plane, and when we reached St. Louis, it was fogged in. So, we circled St. Louis for another hour and a half, and wound up flying to Chicago, where we boarded a bus and slowly journeyed all the way back to St. Louis. It took us a total of thirteen hours to get there, and I listened to this tape the entire time. I rewound and played it literally hundreds of times until I feared it would collapse with fatigue, or the batteries would wear out. But I discovered a great truth. Consciously, we tire of hearing the same thing over and over again, but the subconscious never tires. Repetition simply reinforces the message.

*The next day, I was literally brainwashed with the com-
mands recorded on my tape. I overpowered my opponent
and dominated him as the tape suggested. I pursued him
until the whistle. I started doing things I'd never done before. I rushed the passer early in the game. Just as I was
about to sack him, he released a short pass. The receiver
caught the ball and ran zig-zagging for the goal line. I
pursued even though I normally would have been satisfied
with the pressure I applied to the quarterback, without
chasing the receiver. He was delayed by eluding tacklers
and I tackled him seventy yards downfield. In the film-
study session, the coaches raved about my making a tackle
seventy yards downfield after rushing the quarterback. It
was programmed in so well that it was a reflex action. I
was operating like an efficient robot performing obediently
according to my programming.*

*Maybe that was the norm. I was simply discovering the
mechanism of God's creation. He has equipped me with a
guidance system called the "subconscious." This system is
instructed through the picture-producing brain. These images are stored and played back on cue. What we call
"luck," good or bad, is just the tape we happen to trigger
in the subconscious which plays back just as it went in.
The trick is to put only positive tapes into your mind.
That is the only way to insure your results.*

*Finally, three plays before this game was over, I literally
fainted in exhaustion. But I can honestly say that I've never
played such fantastic football in my life. You see, my subconscious mind had pushed me to carry out the suggestions
on the tape, precisely as I had imagined.*

The Secret Is Application

*JIM: When I first started affirming, "I will be the kind
of man I can respect," I did not want anyone to hear
me saying that. I was afraid people would think I was
trying to be another Norman Vincent Peale. But since
then I've come to understand that using an idea from
somebody else doesn't make you less "yourself." I want
to be the best me I can be. If I learn and apply the
best out of hundreds of lives, so much the better. If it
contributes to my effectiveness, it's great!*

We urge you to take all the best out of this book and any other you can get, and to start applying what you take to your life. Making it part of you won't make you less "you"; it will just make you better and more successful. Just reading this book will not help, even though you may agree it's true.

Clearly state your goals and affirm them several times every day. Picture the achievements as you read them. Feel the emotion of achievement as if it's achieved. Put your goals and affirmations on a cassette with your own voice and listen to the tape. There are few things that benefit us like positive affirmation of our goals on a daily basis. We highly recommend that method of keeping your goals in focus.

LOVING OURSELVES,
ENCOURAGING OTHERS

"You shall love your neighbor as yourself."
—Matthew 22:39, NKJV

You're the greatest! And why are you so great? Because you're human, and human beings are the height of God's creation.

All other of God's creatures either crawl or stoop. Only humans stand upright, looking up toward God. All other creatures have difficulty grasping and holding tools effectively. Only humans have that unique biological feature called the opposing thumb, which helps them to grasp delicately or powerfully as they choose.

Human beings also have vocal cords that can produce fabulous vocabularies far beyond those of any other creature. With those vocal cords, people can sing or speak with tremendous range and precision, communicating countless nuances of thought and feeling.

BILL: As I write, I am in a rather warm room, and there are tiny beads of perspiration dotting my forehead. This reminds me of the unique "air conditioning system" with which God has equipped all of us humans. If we are the least bit warm we perspire, and if we are cold we shiver. We have eyes with over ten million nerve

*cells, and these enable us to see in 3-D living color both
peripherally and straight ahead. Our eyes take constant
"Polaroid" movies that are immediately visible within
the brain.*

We have hearts with over 100,000 miles of veins and
arteries running throughout our bodies. Our hearts pump
blood throughout that 100,000-mile course many times per
day. According to one scientist, one pound of human flesh,
if broken down into its chemical components, would be
worth $570,000,000. If we weigh 150 pounds, our flesh
is worth over $85,000,000,000. This means that each of
us is infinitely valuable! As the psalmist said, we are "fearfully and wonderfully made" (Ps. 139:14).

Our brain is the most amazing instrument of all! It has
over ten billion nerve cells. Even thousands of gigantic
microcomputers cannot duplicate what one human brain
can do, because no computer can program itself. Our
brains *can* program themselves, and they can hold fantastic quantities of data.

If you were to add one bit of information to your memory banks every second for seventy years, you would only
use a small fraction of the storage capacity in the brain
which God has given you. At sixty seconds in a minute,
sixty minutes in an hour, twenty-four hours in a day, seven
days in a week, and fifty-two weeks in a year, that would
be 2,201,472,000 bits of information! The human brain is
a real marvel.

To think about that is exciting because it means God
cared enough about us to give us this special capacity.
He didn't have to, but he must have given it to us for a
reason. Surely he didn't give us that fantastic thinking
ability for it to remain unused.

We would urge you to repeat these words daily until
you accept them as fact: "I'm fantastic because God made
me with the ability to absorb some new bit of information
every second of every minute of every hour of every day
of every week of every year for my entire life. He must
have given me that capacity to use." Then ask, "Well,
what use did he intend for me?" There must be some
good reason for all that ability.

THE FANTASTIC ABILITIES GOD GAVE US

Another reason we humans are fantastic is that God has given us the gift of imagination. That separates us from all other creatures. Pigs are in some ways remarkably like humans. They don't look exactly like us, but they're remarkably similar in the ways their hearts, eyes, ears, lungs, and stomachs function. However, pigs don't have the brain capacity and they don't have the imagination we do. In the most important ways, then, pigs are not at all like humans. But when we don't use those unique gifts of thought and imagination, we become remarkably like pigs!

Donkeys have hearts, lungs, stomachs, ears, eyes, noses. But, like pigs, they don't have anywhere near the brain capacity or the imagination we have. When we don't use our brains and imaginations for goal-oriented work, we're remarkably like donkeys. We must have been given some extra capacities so we wouldn't act or be like pigs and donkeys.

We have the ability to laugh. What other animal has that ability? And we're superior because we have the ability to love—another quality animals don't have. Some animals appear to have something like love, but it's not the same as human love. Animal "love" is primarily instinct; instinct is what makes a mother animal care for her young and fight for it if necessary. But our ability to love is much more than just instinct!

We are superior because we have the ability to encourage other people. Animals don't have this ability. If God has given us this gift to encourage others, he must have intended that we use it.

We also have the God-given ability to empathize. This is the ability to put ourselves in another person's shoes and walk where he walks, or to put ourselves in another person's situation and feel what he feels. (Another definition is the ability to guess what other people are thinking and predict how they will act.) What animal has the ability to empathize?

IT'S OK TO LOVE OURSELVES

Since we as human beings are "fearfully and wonderfully made" creations of God (Ps. 139:14) with many special, God-given abilities, we each should have a great love for ourselves. Of course, we should have an even greater love for our God and for our fellow man, but that doesn't negate the fact that we need to love ourselves, too.

Scripture says that "While we were yet sinners, Christ died for us" (Rom. 5:8). This is PROOF that each of us is important and worthy of love. Is it conceivable that Christ would die for someone unimportant or worthless? He has PROVIDED FOR US fully: "God shall supply all your need according to his riches in glory" (Phil. 4:19)! According to Ephesians 1:3-5, God planned for each of us since the foundation of the world. Is it conceivable that God would promise to provide fully and plan from the foundation of the world for an unimportant person?

Tell yourself, "I am fantastic!" We know that sounds egotistical, but it's not if you keep in mind the *reason* you are fantastic. You are fantastic because God made you and he always does a great job. You are wonderful because he loves you and sent his Son to redeem you. Give God the credit and the glory and you will be able to love yourself without danger of being selfish or egotistical.

The greatest teacher who ever lived, Jesus Christ, was once asked, "What's the most important thing in the world?" He answered with words to this effect: "Love your God and your neighbor as yourself." And he added, "These two are the greatest commandments" (Matt. 22:36-40)!

But actually there are *three* commandments involved here—not two. Loving God is first and all important, and loving your neighbor comes second. But a third commandment is implied in the other two: Love yourself. The Scripture says to love others "as yourself." That means we are to love ourselves, too.

BILL: We can't really love ourselves if we don't love God. Since he made us, we should love that which he made. It is difficult to love the "designer" without loving the "design," too. Many people think that Jesus meant to say, "Love your God, love your neighbor, and hate yourself." But that's not what he said!

If you listen to people, you'll hear them talking about their faults and weaknesses more than anything. They don't give much thought to those things that make them special, unique, and capable; they give most of their thought to what's wrong with them: "I just don't have the enthusiasm he has. I wish I had that much energy. I wish I knew all those things."

Most of us have been taught all our lives to put ourselves down. But not only is that not what God intended; it also keeps us from accomplishing much.

JIM: Privately, on a regular basis, I tell myself, "You're fantastic." I don't say that aloud, because people might misinterpret what I'm doing and think I was being egotistical or selfish. It's never a good idea to brag on ourselves to other people! Nevertheless, I try to keep telling myself quietly that I'm really great. If I were to go around putting myself down, saying things to myself like "You're dumb, stupid, and can't do anything," I would be smothered. Saying things like that would lower my self-image. It would stifle my imagination. But when I tell myself, "You really are terrific," I have a better self-image and am better able to utilize my imagination.

When I tell myself, "You're fantastic" or "You're terrific" or "You're capable," I also tell myself why I am fantastic or terrific or capable. One of the reasons I'm fantastic is that I genuinely like to help people; I'm service minded. Another reason I'm fantastic is that I'm good at helping people achieve their objectives, and that I'm an encourager rather than a discourager. Saying I'm fantastic does not mean I'm arrogant. It means I am acknowledging the fantastic gifts God has given me and thanking him.

Have you ever sat down and made a list of all the things about you that are great? We recommend that you do it. Making a list reminds you of all you have to thank God for and helps you love yourself, because it shows you in writing how many good qualities you have. It also lets you see what qualities you have that can be used to serve and encourage others.

To make a list, sit down and start writing down your strong points—all the ways in which you are special and capable. Think of everything God has enabled you to have, do, or be. Just anything you can think of will be a start— your sense of humor, your ability to communicate, your ability to listen. All these are very important qualities! For instance, listening is a good way to express caring; if we listen with our whole attention, the other person feels valuable and interesting. How often do people give the impression, "I wish you'd hurry up and finish talking because you are boring me"? Being a good listener is a valuable skill to have. If you can honestly put it on your list, you can be very proud and thankful.

The ability to learn is also important. So are the abilities to work, teach, build, and love. We're not going to come up with a totally comprehensive list here. You could spend a long while listing these special, unique, fantastic gifts that God has given you. And you don't have to be limited to the qualities you can think up in one session. You can keep adding to your list as you think of more abilities.

We've found that it is extremely important for us to love ourselves. Telling ourselves positive things and making lists of our strong qualities makes loving ourselves easier. It is really important that we do whatever we can to build up our own self-image, to improve the picture we have of ourselves. This is because we are convinced that all people live, perform, and act in a manner that is consistent with their self-images. All people act, live, and perform in a manner that is consistent with the picture they hold of themselves. So, the better picture we have of ourselves, the better people we are going to be.

OUR DEEP CRAVING TO LOVE OURSELVES

BILL: All of us have a deep, inner craving to love ourselves. The problem is that most people don't really love themselves. This fact is evident in the insecurity of people we meet every day. When it grows to extreme proportions, it causes neuroses and psychoses and other bizarre manifestations. In my prison work, I constantly see people who have been put down all their lives—people who hate themselves and therefore hate other people. Ninety percent of all convicts have been beaten, sexually molested, or otherwise abused when they were children, and this has caused a lot of shame, anger, and self-hate. No wonder they commit terrible crimes!

The need to love oneself is one of the deepest cravings of the human heart. As a result, most people tend to love anyone who helps them love themselves. And they tend to dislike anyone who keeps them from loving themselves. Anyone who tears them down they call "enemy"; anyone who builds them up they call "friend."

When the great coach Vince Lombardi lay dying in a Washington hospital, Willie Davis came to visit him. Willie had been one of the greatest defensive ends who ever lived. He had played for Lombardi during the glory days at Green Bay in the mid-60s. Now he had come all the way from the West Coast to say goodbye to his old coach.

When Willie came out of the hospital room, there were several reporters waiting. They asked, "Willie—Mr. Davis—why did you come?" Willie answered, "None of your business," and walked away. They followed him downstairs, where he waited for a cab. And they kept on asking, "Willie, tell us why you did it. You traveled across an entire continent to visit that man. Why?" Willie still refused to answer. He got into a cab that had pulled up to the curb.

As the cab pulled away, the writers were still yelling after him, "Willie—Mr. Davis—why did you feel you had to come?" Willie stuck his head out of the cab window and yelled back, "That man made me feel important!" Most people would go all the way across America or halfway around the world for anyone who makes them feel that way!

BILL: Now, we're not trying to say we should help people love themselves and feel important just so they will love us and do things for us. We're just trying to show how great a need people have to feel worthwhile and worthy of love. Some people will do almost anything for attention that might help them feel a little more important.

I was recently in Chicago and saw a man dressed up in a stupid-looking red Spiderman suit. He placed suction cups on his hands and feet to climb the side of one of the tallest buildings in the world. He climbed 125 stories! When he came over the top, there was a group of writers and policemen waiting for him. They asked, "Why in the world would you risk your life climbing up this tall building?" He said, "I like to see my name in the paper."

This need for attention and appreciation starts when we are children. I remember my boys would come in when they were quite young and ask me to come out and play ball with them. I would go outside to play football, basketball, baseball—any game they wanted. As they grew older, they still wanted me to come out, but they really weren't all that interested in my playing with them. They just wanted me to watch and brag on them!

It seems to us that one of the main jobs any parent has is to brag on his kids and make them feel worthwhile. In fact, we would even say that the art of good parenting is the art of praising children! Too many people try to catch their children doing something wrong. We feel it's better to try to catch our children doing something right, and to compliment them for it. Much of what is called constructive criticism is not really constructive. It is often destructive! Many parents are so preoccupied with teaching their children humility that they fail to teach them confidence.

BILL: At one point while they were growing up, both my sons played for the same assistant coach. And they couldn't stand him! They said he was the dumbest, stupidest, most horrible coach they had ever played for. I asked them why they thought he was so bad. After some probing, I discovered he was always putting them down, pointing out their mistakes, and picking on them. He never failed to point out their failures.

My boys told me they hated this coach. Of course, I tried to point out that they shouldn't really hate him. Finally, after some long discussion, I managed to change their opinions. They now announced, "We hate his guts!" (Hating someone's guts is worse than just

*hating them.) Why did they feel so bad about this coach?
Because he always pointed out their mistakes and failures, and never noticed anything they did right.*

*Grant Teaff, another coach both my sons played for,
was a man whom they thought was the most intelligent
of all coaches. They loved him, and the main reason
was that he was always pointing out their successes,
always building them up. In his mind, they were all-
American, all-pro, all-world. And he made them feel
that they were really worthwhile. As a result, they loved
him and played their best for him.*

Being Encouragers

If we have a healthy self-love, we also feel a great
thankfulness to God for all he's done for us. After all,
he made us, and he has loved, listened to, given to, and
taught us. In appreciation for his goodness, we are moved
to try to benefit others. And because other people have
such a deep need to love themselves, one of the best ways
we can benefit others is to love them, encourage them,
and help them love themselves.

There are countless ways we can do this. Telling our
wives that we love them and backing up those words with
action makes them feel good and can help give them a
better self-image. So can telling our husbands how much
we appreciate them. Telling our children that we love them
and treating them in a loving manner does wonders.

*JIM: Often, when I see people who look just a little
"down in the dumps," I try to say something to build
them up. If I know them well enough, I can be very
direct. I walk up to them and say something like, "You
know what? I really think you're fantastic." They usually light up like lightbulbs! I see sadness or indifference
changed as if by a miracle to renewed zest for life.*

*To a woman, I sometimes say, "You know what? I
think you're beautiful." But I have found it's usually
best to comment on character traits rather than on
physical appearance. For instance, I might say, "I notice you have a beautiful combination of intelligence*

and talent." I also find that being very specific adds weight to the encouraging word. Rather than saying, "I think you are great," I might say, "Your patience with that mischievous little neighbor child makes it obvious to me that you are very kind and loving."

The skillful, sensitive compliment is one important key to helping other people love themselves. Of course, the more sincere and believable the encouragement, the more effective it will be. Like sunflowers, which follow the sun with their faces all day long, people turn toward you if you pick out their strengths and express sincere appreciation for those strengths.

What if we never stopped to think about that fantastic, unique ability that God has given us to love, empathize, encourage, and uplift? Isn't it a waste and a shame when something so fantastic goes unused?

Remember, the urge to help and encourage others grows out of a strong sense of gratitude to God for the gifts he has given us. Obviously, the reverse happens when we stop focusing on what God has done and focus only on ourselves. Healthy self-love is not selfish! It is God-centered, not self-centered.

When we think about ourselves too much, all those situations that ought to remind us to help others become aggravations to us. The fact that someone is down in the dumps should say to us, "Here's a great opportunity to encourage." But if we're all involved with ourselves instead of focusing on God's goodness, we will just be irritated when we see others unhappy.

When a person doesn't know something, we should be thinking, "I can teach him." But if we're not thinking right, if our focus is on ourselves, we say to ourselves, "That guy is stupid. Why doesn't the dummy do anything right?"

Whenever we find that we're irritated with someone, upset with someone, or running someone down, we have a good indication that our minds are on ourselves, not on the other person—and certainly not on God. When we see someone who needs to know something, do we seek to fill his need or call him a dummy? When we see someone

who hates himself, do we seek to help him love himself,
or do we say, "Look at the things that guy is doing. He's
no good!" Our reaction to other people's needs is a good
indicator of whether we are focusing on God and responding in gratitude for all he has done or simply focusing
on ourselves.

HELPING OTHERS BENEFITS US, TOO

One really exciting thing about helping others love
themselves is that it helps us, too. God has set up his
universe in such a way that, as we benefit the lives of
others, we benefit. Spencer Hays's grandmother, a very
wise lady, constantly quotes Edwin Markham, who said,
"There's a destiny that makes us brothers; none goes his
way alone. Whatever we put into the lives of others will
return into our own lives." So, building up others and
encouraging them will result in our being built up and
encouraged as well. We only get back what we put out.
So if we don't build others up, we won't have anything
coming back to us that uplifts us in return.

If we have a lot of money, isn't it better to put the
money in a savings account than just to store it in a vault?
If we put it in a savings account, it will be used; the
bank will loan our money out to other people for purposes
such as building houses. And the savings account will
accrue interest. Your savings will grow because your
money is put to use. We will end up with more money
than we started with.

We all have many fantastic abilities. We can use them
and have them grow like the savings account, and everything we put in will be credited to us. All those things
we do will come back to us.

In Luke 6:31, Jesus said, "As ye would that men should
do to you, do ye also to them likewise"—this is the Golden
Rule. We should be eager to help others, not because of
what we are going to get in return, but because it's the
right thing to do and that which gives us a blessing! However, this verse indicates and human experience proves
that what we do for others frequently does come back
to us. Luke 6:38 says, "Give, and it shall be given unto

you; good measure, pressed down, and shaken together, and running over, shall men give unto you." This passage teaches that, as we give to others, in that same measure will we receive. Our return will be proportionate to our giving!

Our ability to contribute to other people is pivotal. And the motivation to help others comes from a healthy self-love and an appreciation for God's goodness to us. When we think about him and all he has done for us, we want to do what will benefit others.

Now, if we didn't remind ourselves of this, we would forget. So we suggest that you add another step when you work on your list of strong points—the things that make you fantastic. As you list each God-given asset, take a clean sheet of paper and write that asset at the top of the page. Then start listing all the ways you can use that asset to benefit other people, to encourage and uplift them. You probably will come up with 100, 200, or even 300 ideas for ways to help others. Then use those lists as guides and reminders of things you can do to build up your family, your friends, your associates—even people you meet casually.

TELL YOURSELF POSITIVE THINGS

One of the greatest, most successful salesmen that I've ever known was a life-insurance salesman named Ben Feldman. One of the rules he lived by was to constantly work at selling himself on what he was doing. He was always selling himself on the life insurance business. And he was continually selling himself on New York Life, the company whose insurance he sold.

Having the right attitude about ourselves, the people around us, and our profession is extremely important. This is because what we like or dislike—and whether we are happy or not—will depend on what we decide about these things. Circumstances won't determine whether we like our situation or not. It's our attitude that will make the difference.

JIM: I like some people I used to dislike. I enjoy doing some things I used to hate. The reason I like those people

I used to dislike is that I changed my attitude about those people. I changed my attitude about those things I hated to do.

I first learned this principle when I was selling books and Bibles with the Southwestern Company during the summers while I was in college. It was a great experience—a crash course in selling. The company taught me that it was good to tell myself positive things about the people on whom I was going to call. They said,

> *Tell yourself, "The finest people in the whole world live right around here, and I'm going to be selling to them today. They are really nice people." When you talk to them, tell them how fine they are. If in advance you say, "Man, these are going to be a bunch of obnoxious, nasty people today," what you think about them will be reflected in your attitude toward them. But if you say, "The finest people in the world live in this neighborhood and I'm going to get to call on some of them," your attitude will be the best.*

Say good things about yourself. Say good things about your job and your company and your profession. Say good things about the people with whom you come in contact. You can prepare for a great attitude by saying to yourself things like, "The greatest thing I can do is get to deal with these fantastic people! My customers are wonderful, warm, and open to me!" Or, "My work as a homemaker is worthwhile and fulfilling. I have the most wonderful family in the world, and they depend on me." Or, "This is the best school in the city. The teachers really care about me and want to help me learn."

JIM: If there is some aspect of your situation you find unpleasant, try saying good things about that, too. When I first started working for Spencer Hays, I was very aware of the fact that he was very successful and I wasn't. So I started wanting to learn from him. But on occasion I also found myself being jealous of him. I soon found a way to handle these feelings of jealousy. The moment I felt even a twinge of jealousy, I would immediately say to myself, "I'm going to help Spencer have everything he wants and more. I'm going to con-

tribute to his success, so that if he wants to have five cars, I'll help him get them. If he wants homes in the United States, France, and England, I'm going to help get them for him." It is hard to be jealous of someone whom you are trying to help become more successful. Instead of feeling jealous or negative toward Spencer, I instantly replaced these feelings with their opposites.

Don't ever knock yourself, your company, your product, your prospects, or your customers. That doesn't mean you should overlook something wrong that needs to be changed. You can make constructive recommendations, but keep your attitude positive.

We've seen people get together to gripe, whine, and complain. All they did was make things worse. What they could have done was tell someone who could do something about the problem, or get together and say, "Let's figure out how to solve this situation." If a solution was out of the range of their authority, they could still have come up with suggestions and ideas and presented those ideas to the person who would have the authority to change the situation.

SAYING AND THINKING

It is important to think positive thoughts. But saying our positive statements aloud is even more effective. Speaking aloud helps keep our minds focused. We can talk on one subject for thirty minutes and hardly think about any other subject. But it is hard to think about one subject for more than five minutes without being severely distracted.

If you are not sure about this, try an experiment. Try to see just how long you can think about one subject without saying anything out loud about it. You will find your mind wandering. But when you talk about the same subject, your mind will not wander.

When it comes to positive thoughts, what you say is what you get. But your positive thoughts, like every other part of your life, should relate to your goals.

JIM: I keep going back to my 3 x 5 cards to remind myself of my goals so I can make positive statements about them. My cards remind me of so many things I want to say, think, and do, and I carry some with me all the time. Now, I can't reasonably carry all my cards all the time. So I carry some of them for a month, use some different ones the next month, and then change to still another set for the third month. But all my goals are also written in my notebook so I can open the book at any time and read them.

It is especially important at all times for us to remember who we are—the highest of God's creatures, and individuals to whom God has given many special and valuable characteristics. We are fantastic. *You* are fantastic! Keep reminding yourself of that fundamental truth. Remember to encourage others and help them understand that they are fantastic, too. And then keep writing your goals, writing your lists of GO work. Vocalize, visualize, and feel the emotion of what you want to do. Keep your focus on what you want to achieve. You are on your way toward being a winner!

KEEPING SCORE

"So then each one of us shall give account
of himself to God."—Romans 14:12, NAS

BILL: Blanton Collier, who was head coach of the Cleveland Browns while I was playing during the 1960s, was a football genius! He knew that keeping the score was extremely important. And he discovered that even players who don't score touchdowns need to be able to keep up with how they're doing. Of course, the score at the end of the game was the score to which he gave the most attention, but he also kept score on all the intricate details of individual and team play. Every offensive and defensive play and all the players who made them had a separate score.

It's difficult to grade a defensive end, the position I played. However, Collier devised a most ingenious system. It is the primary job of the defensive lineman to rush the quarterback. Naturally, the ultimate accomplishment for such a player is sacking the quarterback (tackling him for a loss). But there are many occasions when a defensive lineman would not actually throw the quarterback for a loss, but would distract or hurry him as he was getting ready to throw a pass. This would

*cause an interception or incomplete pass, and obviously
this result was also desirable.*

*So, Collier decided to give credit to linemen who made
what he called "first forces." To make a "first force,"
a player would have to be the first lineman to break
through the blockers, get to the quarterback, and distract him or cause him to throw the ball too quickly.
Collier gave a great deal of credit to linemen who did
this. He also kept up with the number of tackles each
defensive lineman made on running downs and the
number of assisted tackles he made. The lineman who
had a great many sacks, first forces, tackles, and assisted tackles was naturally considered to be a better
lineman than the ones who didn't. An even more complex system was used to grade offensive linemen.*

*The average fan doesn't know how pivotal the line-
man is to the success of the team. But Collier did, and
he graded every play. Every guard or tackle (whose
name was probably unfamiliar to most fans) had a
score on each play.*

*I will never forget the year this intricate grading sys-
tem was instituted on our team. It put a whole new
zest into the game for me! I was sad if we didn't win,
but I still had a feeling of accomplishment concerning
my own performance if my "score" showed a lot of tackles, assisted tackles, first forces, and sacks. If we won,
and I didn't have those good statistics—that bothered
me as well. It was a constant motivation to me to score
high on those stats, regardless of whether we won or
lost.*

*After out-of-town games, we would all climb on a bus
and go to the airport to catch our chartered plane home.
The official game statistics would be circulated on the
bus; these were the statistics that had been kept in the
press box. The backs would anxiously read those statistic
sheets. But the only statistics kept in the press box for
linemen were sacks and tackles. So we always looked
forward to the more complete statistic sheet we would
see on Tuesday morning at the film-study session. This
is where we saw Coach Collier's statistics, which in-
cluded other measurements that related to linemen,*

such as first forces and assisted tackles. These stats were posted on the bulletin board for everyone to see. That was important, because it made everyone accountable for his own score.

Needless to say, if everyone scored high in all the stats, we usually won. Even in a team sport, individual play is important. The composite of good play by each player is a winning team effort!

You may have noticed that scoreboards in football stadiums are getting larger and more complex every year. Literally millions of dollars are spent on these scoreboards. At a basketball game, the scoreboard covers a large percentage of the area above the court. Those huge scoreboards include all the individual and team statistics, as well as keep track of the score and playing time. In baseball, the statistics are kept in surprisingly meticulous detail. Keeping score is important in every sport. If you remove scorekeeping from sports, those sports would be a lot less interesting. And we believe the athletes would not perform nearly as well without the scores.

KEEPING SCORE IS NOT JUST FOR SPORTS

But sports isn't the only area of endeavor where keeping score is important. For instance, there is no doubt that people in business do better if they know a score is being kept. There is an old management adage that "people do what you *in*spect, not what you *ex*pect." We would amend that to say, "people do what you *in*spect, *as well as* what you *ex*pect." But we would still agree that inspection—grading or keeping score—in a business helps motivate employees and keep them working at full capacity.

JIM: I used to be a teacher. And the single most frustrating thing for me about teaching was not being able to measure my performance—to keep score. I could never tell, to my satisfaction, how I was doing. If the principal had come in every month or six weeks and given the kids a reliable test, perhaps I could have seen their progress. If they were doing better, then I could have said, "I'm doing well. I'm helping them. They are responding to my teaching." But the system didn't work

that way. In teaching there were no visible scoreboards.
And that made teaching difficult for me.

Frank Bettger, in his book, *How I Raised Myself from*
Failure to Success in Selling, says that he achieved
great success in selling only after applying some key principles he had learned in baseball. One of the most important of these principles is that in sales the score must
be kept carefully and fairly. It's also important to publish the score constantly. People need to know where they
stand!

One of the reasons keeping score is so important is
that it helps people keep track of their progress toward
their goals. In sales, good companies publish the sales
reports—that's keeping score! The salesmen have a quota
to meet, and measuring how each salesman does in relation to his quota is a way of keeping score. Salesmen
have a pay plan—and determining what they make is another form of scorekeeping.

KEEPING SCORE ON OURSELVES

Because keeping score is so important for letting us
see how we stand in relation to our goals, it's best not
to rely on letting others keep score for us. Each of us
should keep score on ourselves—and we should keep it
by different and higher standards than would ever be
asked of us by others. If we only do that which other
people ask of us, we will not accomplish anything near
what we could accomplish.

Our standards should be set in keeping with those fantastic abilities we talked about in the previous chapter.
If we make a list of those abilities and keep score on
ourselves according to how we use them, we will set a
much higher standard for ourselves than anyone would
ever expect of us.

JIM: As great as Spencer Hays is, he would have asked
too little of me as a salesman, a sales manager, and
then president of Tom James. He wouldn't have had
the guts to be demanding enough. I believe a person
needs to keep score on himself so he can plot his own
progress according to his own personal goals.

A good sales manager is always trying to get his sales-people to do their best. But his is a tricky position. He can't afford to let his people get sloppy, but neither does he want to put so much pressure on his people that he short-circuits their effectiveness with overstress. So he probably puts a lot less pressure on them than they would put on themselves.

BILL: A father is in much the same position. He wants to get the best out of his children, but he can't afford to push too hard. When my sons were in elementary school, they wanted to play little-league football. I refused to let them. One reason was that I was afraid they would have bad coaching from frustrated "Vince Lombardis" who had probably never played the game, but who thought themselves to be great coaches. I felt it would be better for my sons to learn right the first time from a good coach. But, more important, I feared that they would get burned out and lose their enthusiasm for the game before they ever started junior-high-school football.

As time went on, I discovered an even more important reason not to let my boys play while they were so young. I was a pro football player, and this put a great deal of pressure on my sons also to be players. I wanted to protect them from this pressure until they were old enough to handle it.

Rather than killing my sons' enthusiasm, my refusing to let them play too soon built their excitement for the day when they would be allowed to play. When they entered junior high and were allowed to play, they were so determined that they soon caught up with their friends who had been playing little league for years. Ultimately, they far surpassed most of their classmates. Some of those kids who had been playing little-league ball for years quit before they got through high school. They were tired of football. Anyone who motivates other people must take extreme care that the attempt at motivation is really effective.

It's helpful to have other people keep score for us. In fact, we're fortunate if we have even one person who talks to us on a regular basis about achieving up to our potential. However, if we reach only the level that other people expect of us, the level of our achievement will be low. The score we keep for ourselves should be based on our aspirations, not on what other people expect. So we hope other people are keeping score on us. But we also try to remember that we are our own best score-keeper.

It doesn't really matter to us what other people say we're doing. Every now and then someone compliments us, and if we know we didn't do our best, the compliment doesn't make us happy. On occasions when we know we have done our dead-level best but nobody has complimented us, we still have the good feeling of knowing our score is good.

JIM: I can't imagine not entering checks in my checkbook. Keeping tabs on the checks I write keeps me from overdrawing my account. What if I made deposits and the bank didn't credit those deposits to me? I wouldn't like that at all. It's of great importance to keep our checkbooks right. But it is even more important to keep score on ourselves. And I'm not just talking about keeping score on our business goals! It is important to keep track of the progress we are making in all our goals—those concerning our Christian lives, our families, our professions, and our health.

How to Keep Score

It's important for us to have high goals for ourselves in every major area of our lives. And the score we keep on ourselves should be based on whether or not we're moving toward those objectives. Even if no one ever sees our scorecards, we still need to keep score diligently, faithfully, and honestly—every day. It's not something we're doing to impress others, but a tool to help us keep on track toward reaching our goals.

If you are in sales, for instance, keeping score would mean keeping track of how many people you actually talked to and asked for an appointment. To how many people did you try to sell? How many genuine prospects did you locate? Again, the purpose of such scorekeeping is not to put down a number that satisfies someone you would like to impress. The point is keeping score for yourself and studying that score. The scoresheet will show when you are doing well, and will also help you pinpoint problem areas. For instance, if you're coming up with a good number of prospects but not getting enough appointments, your scoresheet may reveal that you are not calling on enough people.

Suppose your goal is to lose twenty-five pounds. The same principle applies. Keeping accurate records of how much you weigh each day, how much you eat, and how much exercise you get can help you pinpoint reasons why your weight isn't declining as fast as you would like. Maybe the problem is that bowl of ice cream you like to eat before going to bed. Or maybe you've been too busy to exercise. Keeping score on yourself lets you see what's wrong and take steps to remedy the situation so you can continue to progress toward your goals.

Now, the method you use to keep score on yourself depends on you—and on what your goals are. If your progress can be measured in numerical terms—such as pounds lost or sales made—you can keep track of your progress on a graph. It's a good idea to start low and plot the graph toward intermediate goals. Then, after that, you can plot to a higher level. As you achieve your goals, you can see your progress on to a higher level.

JIM: I use a much simpler method to keep track of my progress toward my business goals. Once again, I make use of those 3 x 5 cards. I always carry around a card with the figure for my best month written on it. Then, when I have beaten that best-month figure, I mark through it and write down the new achievement. Then I set a new, higher goal for myself.

Of course, some goals can't be measured in numerical amounts, but you can still keep score on them. One way is to make lists in your notebook of things you have achieved that have brought you nearer to your goals. Or when you complete a task listed under "GO work," you can mark out that task and write down a new one. The whole process of reviewing your goals and listing new GO activities can be a form of keeping score.

Don't Let Yourself Fall Back

We should always be progressing toward our goals. That is one reason for keeping score—so we can keep ourselves from falling back. Some people would say, "Well, you can't beat your previous records all the time." Why not? There is no reason we can't continuously do our best or even better than our best. And this doesn't mean that we should work longer and longer hours. We should be able to work the same number of hours and still get better all the time, because we're improving our skills and abilities. If we keep learning and improving, we can continue to better our goals without putting out more and more effort.

The thing we must decide is: "I'm not going to fall back. I'm going to keep going forward!" When we do this, we will constantly be making progress. And when that happens, we will be encouraged to keep on working for more progress. It is discouraging not to move ahead. If we don't make progress, it is hard for us to stay motivated. And lack of progress tends to make us insecure.

Another thing that tends to happen when we don't make progress toward our goals is that we begin to make excuses and to blame others. We start saying things like, "I can't lose weight because I've got big bones." Or, "The reason I'm not selling better is that the economy is bad. How could I expect to sell more when my manager doesn't sell as well as I do? He's been in the business longer than I have." Such excuses keep us from taking personal responsibility.

As we keep score on ourselves, we must determine we are not going to fall backward—no matter what. And we must take responsibility for our own progress. One of the great things that will happen when we do this is that we will begin to judge ourselves on the basis of our goals. When we make progress toward our goals, we will look good to other scorekeepers. But if we've set our own goals and kept our own score we will look great to ourselves. Progress is wonderful for our self-esteem!

Faith at Work

Every one of us performs in a manner consistent with our own self-image. And our self-image can't ever be all it should be until we see our potential the way God sees it. We should try to get a glimpse of what God thinks we're capable of and base our goal-setting and scorekeeping on that. All human beings think small compared to God. He says, "According to your faith be it unto you" (Matt. 9:29). In essence, he is saying, "The only thing holding you back is your lack of faith!"

If you honestly had faith that you could not fail, if there was no place in your thinking for failure, if you absolutely knew you would win—and win big—what would your goals be? God honors faith and he will bless and empower you when you have this type of faith—provided you are keeping in touch with him and not trying to accomplish things that are out of keeping with his plans for you.

Have you ever given any thought to what it would take to reach your big, "unreachable" goals? Try making a list, and keep adding to that list your ideas about what might be done to enable you to reach these big goals. Write down everything; otherwise your best ideas could be lost forever. And look over your list from time to time. Let your subconscious work on it, even while you are applying your conscious mind to your smaller, more immediate goals. You may be surprised at how quickly your "impossible" goal starts to seem possible.

JIM: I started working for Tom James in 1965. I started formulating my goals and writing them down in late 1967. For those first two-and-a-half years I had been inspired by what I was learning, but I hadn't had any concept of what it was that made successful people succeed and failures fail. Much of what I have talked about in this book I didn't understand at all. But late in 1967, when I put down in writing that I would help build Tom James to become a $100,000,000 business, one of the things I included in my goal was that I would personally figure out how to sell $1,000,000 worth of

*clothing myself. I started making a list of things I would
do. Shortly thereafter I became director of sales for Tom
James. I really believe that if I hadn't been pushing
toward an "impossible" goal I probably would never
have become director of sales. And had I not become
director of sales and continued to think about how I
could help build the company to a $100,000,000 in sales,
I don't think I would be chairman of the board and
CEO of Tom James today.*

*If I hadn't started keeping score by different stan-
dards, then I might have "flunked out" of the business.
If I had only done what someone else asked of me, he
wouldn't have asked enough for me to move ahead the
way I have. But I continue to ask even more of myself
because I try to set high goals and have the faith to
work toward them.*

HOLD YOURSELF ACCOUNTABLE

Two of the biggest causes for failure to reach goals
are alcohol and drugs. They become an escape or a chemical ego trip. But rationalization and dishonesty in keeping
score often put an even worse drag on accomplishment.
How often do we figure our failure escape routes even
before we start? How often do we "cheat" just a little
in keeping score on ourselves? How often do we give excuses or blame others for our failure to make progress
toward our goals?

But these little tricks are just ways of fooling ourselves.
No matter how we try, we can't escape a basic truth:
We are accountable for what we do. We are accountable
to our company for the return we make on the salary
invested in us. We are accountable to our families for
carrying out our responsibilities to them. And even if other
people don't hold us accountable, we are ultimately accountable to ourselves and to God.

It is really impossible to keep a secret. Our deception—
even of ourselves—is at best only very brief. Luke 12:3
says, "Therefore whatsoever ye have spoken in darkness
shall be heard in the light; and that which ye have spoken
in the ear in closets shall be proclaimed upon the house-

tops." Anything we do will sooner or later come to light—
in this life or in the one to come. For instance, if we cheat
sexually, we run the risk of venereal disease or pregnancy.
And even if penicillin or the pill could help us out, we
still couldn't avoid the fear, guilt, and personal torment.
Besides, no matter how careful we are, people *do* find
out about these things, even when we think we've taken
steps to make sure no one will know.

In the long run, even though we may attempt to deceive
ourselves, we always know when we are not being everything we should be. And this lowers ourselves in our own
eyes. It's like a man ignoring his faithful barking dog
as thieves come in and steal, or a woman shutting her
eyes to an illness until it is too late to treat it. We may
think we're escaping our problems by ignoring them, but
we're not. In the final analysis, we just can't hide anything
from ourselves.

Most foolish of all is to think we can hide from God.
In Luke 12 it is pointed out that God knows us so well
that he knows the number of hairs on our heads! Authorities tell us that blondes have about 145,000 hairs, dark-
haired people have 120,000, and redheads have about
90,000. Obviously, this information is a hopeless piece of
trivia; you may even feel it is too unimportant for us to
include in this book. But God is saying in this passage
that even these unimportant details are known to him.
We must never forget that he is even more concerned
with what we do. The passage goes on to say that God
knows when a sparrow falls. Sparrows are of little worth
compared with humans. So God is very interested in what
happens to us. And the fact that he sent his Son to die
for us proves we are of limitless value to him.

GOD KEEPS SCORE

God knows each of us and cares about us, but he keeps
score, too. He holds us accountable. We can rationalize
and blame our lack of progress on other people, Satan,
or anyone else, but there is no escaping the fact that
we must stand before God in judgment and be held respon-
sible for what we have done with our lives.

When John Hinckley shot President Reagan, the shooting was shown and reshown on television for the world to see. But amazingly, Hinckley was held by the courts to be mentally ill and therefore unaccountable. God doesn't let us off like this. His grace is sufficient for our forgiveness, if we repent, but he never just lets us off the hook.

It is almost impossible to lose motivation in our important goals when we realize we are utterly accountable to God. The impossibility of secrecy and the reality of total accountability makes sin not only foolish and unprofitable, but absolutely stupid.

It is important to understand the extent of this accountability. Matthew 12:36 says that "Every idle word that men shall speak, they shall give account thereof in the day of judgment." Just as his knowledge is so detailed as to include "the number of the hairs in our heads," our accountability is so complete as to include "every idle word." And we will be accountable not so much for our words' beauty or wisdom, but for their honesty and purity!

First John 3:17 says, "But whoso hath this world's good, and seeth his brother have need, and shutteth up his bowels of compassion from him, how dwelleth the love of God in him?" This tells us that it should be impossible for us to step over human need, if we say that the love of God dwells in us. The Bible further teaches us that God favors helping those who are helpless—the widowed, the orphaned, the imprisoned. But it also teaches that the greatest help we can give is spiritual. If you feed a hungry man you may satisfy him for one meal. But if you introduce him to Jesus Christ, the Bread of Life, and he experiences a spiritual rebirth, he will live forever!

How God Keeps Score

If God keeps such careful score—and the Scriptures teach us that he does—we need to know: by what standards? It is obvious that he keeps score differently than man does. In the business world, if a person makes a lot of money, he is considered a success. But God's standards are different. The rich young ruler is a good example of the difference between human standards and God's standards. This man had all the outer trappings of success, but in the eyes of God he was a failure.

God does not keep score on us according to how "religious" we act. In fact, Jesus was most critical of the scribes and Pharisees, the most "religious people" of his day, because he said they were like "whited sepulchres." A sepulchre was a burial place above ground for the dead, and was usually made of stucco. Many sepulchres were painted to look stark white and beautiful on the outside. But Christ pointed out that on the inside, these structures were full of dead men's bones. People who only act "religious," who seem white and beautiful on the outside but are corrupt on the inside, nauseate the Lord.

Jesus also said that we don't get right with God by doing good works—although he certainly wants us to do good works. Ephesians 2:8–9 says, "For by grace are ye saved through faith; and that not of yourselves: it is the gift of God: *Not* of works, lest any man should boast" (italics added). God's scorekeeping is not a matter of works—we are saved by grace through faith. We are saved when we believe, not having seen. We become God's when we accept his unmerited favor, which was the death, burial, and resurrection of Jesus Christ on the cross.

In Romans 10:3, Paul says, "For they being ignorant of God's righteousness, and going about to establish their own righteousness, have not submitted themselves unto the righteousness of God." People who are ignorant of God's righteousness, set about to pile up their own righteousness. As a result, they never submit themselves to the righteousness of God, which is Christ. As long as we are trying to substitute our own goodness, we never get right with God.

Too many of us think that what we need to do to become right with God is allow him to supply about 20 percent of his righteousness, with 80 percent of our own. (Some wicked criminal might have to supply only 20 percent of his righteousness and God would have to supply the remaining 80 percent.) But the Bible says we don't need *any* of our own righteousness. We need an altogether different kind of righteousness—the kind that Christ provided when he died and rose again.

As long as we trust in ourselves and our own goodness, we never get right with God. It is only as we are willing to throw ourselves helplessly upon the grace of God that we really get right with him.

We must always keep it firmly in mind that we are totally accountable to God. In Romans 14:12, Paul says, "So then every one of us shall give account of himself to God." We will be accountable not only for our works and words, but for our priorities, according to 2 Peter 3:10, which says that the Lord is going to come in a great, cataclysmic judgment to destroy the world by fire, and that only those things we have done that are spiritual will last. All of our houses, land, and money will mean nothing. All we'll be left with is a pile of ashes.

This passage certainly helps us keep our priorities straight! It shows us that whatever can be burned with fire will vanish. Keep in mind that this fire is the fire of God, and it can burn through safety-deposit boxes and bank vaults. The only things that can't burn are those spiritual things we have done—and all those we have introduced to Jesus Christ. God's fire won't burn down spiritual treasures we have laid up in heaven!

There will be little comfort in comparing ash piles where our houses and earthly valued possessions were kept. The Bible says in Luke 12:20, ". . . Thou fool, this night thy soul shall be required of thee: then whose shall those things be, which thou hast provided?" God is saying that the ultimate accountability is for our souls. "What is a man profited, if he shall gain the whole world, and lose his own soul or what shall a man give in exchange for his soul?" (Matt. 16:26). If we get the whole world and lose our soul, we make a bad deal! Only fools go about their workaday activities with no concern for their souls.

ACCOUNTABILITY IS A SOURCE OF ENCOURAGEMENT

It is an awesome thing to realize the extent of our accountability to God. But to the Christian that accountability should be a source of encouragement, not fear. God holds us accountable because he knows each of us and cares about us. He is intimately involved in our affairs. And that should give us a great deal of hope and joy.

People tend to fall apart when they think no one knows or cares about them. When a person feels as if he makes no difference to anyone, he may even become suicidal, thinking "If no one knows or cares, then no one could possibly love me. And if no one loves me, what difference does it make whether I live or die?" If a person loses total hope, doctors tell us, he will die within three days.

But the good news is that there *is* hope! God knows and cares about each of us. He loves us more than any human being possibly can. And that is why he is interested in everything we do. Hebrews 12:1 says that every person who has died in Christ and is now in heaven is watching from heaven's grandstand, cheering our victories and lamenting our defeats. There are literally billions watching us from heaven! And Luke 16 teaches that even those in hell are watching and are concerned that we make the right decisions, that we not suffer the horror of that terrible place. If those in heaven and hell and, most important, God himself, all watch us so intently, each of us must realize that we are of great value. That should be a source of great hope and encouragement for us.

BILL: Knowing how much God cares about us should cause us to run toward God, not away from him. I remember when I was just a boy and would do something I shouldn't. I would run, but it did no good; my dad would always catch me. He was a fine athlete, a pro baseball pitcher, and he whipped with his open hand. He was a left-hander, and he could tan my seat good!

I soon discovered that it was much better to run to my father when I had been wrong, to yell, "I'm sorry, I'm sorry!" and to hug him. If I ran away, I always caught it right where it did the most good. But if I ran to him and hugged him and said, "I'm sorry," I seldom got a whipping.

There are two reasons my father couldn't whip me when I did that. The first was psychological: it's tough to whip a kid who's hugging you and saying he's sorry. The second was purely physical: you can't get leverage on someone who's hugging you!

All too often, our natural instinct is to run away from

our heavenly Father who loves us and holds us accountable. But the wise move is to run to him and ask forgiveness.

Once forgiven, we are free to keep on progressing. We are able to keep setting new goals for our spiritual life, our families, our professions, and our health. We are given imagination to visualize success and discipline to focus in on our goals. We are given the emotional resources to commit ourselves to our goals, the perseverance to adequately prepare ourselves and to do GO work. And we are given the positive resources to affirm our goals constantly, to encourage ourselves and to use our fantastic abilities to encourage others.

If we do all these things while keeping in close relationship with our heavenly Father, we will be progressing in our main goal: to do his will. And if we continue toward that goal, we can be sure that our heavenly Father will be pleased with our score!